What Your Colleagues Are Saying . . .

"Now that the real work of NGSS implementation has begun, there is a high demand for quality instructional resources that show how core ideas and concepts, practices, and the nature of science come together in meaningful, intellectually engaging science investigations supported with content and pedagogical background information for the teacher. Thank you, Alan Colburn, for providing a resource that addresses the challenges and practical reality of transitioning to quality classroom instruction that mirrors our current best thinking about teaching and learning science."

—Page Keeley
Past President of the National Science Teachers Association

"A lot of research points to elementary teachers not feeling comfortable with science education because they don't have strong background knowledge in science. This book provides an easy to understand method of teaching elementary students how to do science. The sample activities and implementation pointers will help novice teachers approach science education in a thoughtful manner."

—Ryan McDonnell, EdD
Assistant Principal, Animo Jackie
Robinson Charter High School

"Most books of this sort concentrate on theory. This one includes practice, and well thought out and explained examples of how to get your students to meet the chapters' objectives . . . Elementary teachers may do little to no science teaching that doesn't involve reading the book and answering the questions. This is a 'how to' manual for hands-on, minds-on science inquiry."

—Deanna Brunlinger
NBCT Science Teacher, Science Department Chair,
Elkhorn Area High School

"I think this would be a great book for college classes in teacher education. Future teachers can think about this before ever beginning teaching and go into [it] with the expectation that this *is* how they should approach science teaching."

—Mandy Frantti
Teacher, Munising Public Schools

"Many science teachers are struggling when planning using the NGSS. The alignment is not evident. This book shows how to establish connections between science content and the standards (NGSS)."

—*Rosario Canizales, PhD*
Science Lead Teacher,
Irene C. Hernandez Middle School

"The classroom practitioner's path to authentic, effective science teaching is littered with cast-off 'how-to' manuals that are too dense, too pedantic, and too variable. Not in this case. Dr. Alan Colburn builds meaningful context using familiar and accessible activities in a relatable, charmingly modest conversational tone, equipping elementary and middle school science teachers with a trifecta—a firm grounding in the key tenets of science, immediately deliverable classroom activities, and alignment to the Next Generation Science Standards."

—*Jeff Weld, PhD*
Executive Director, Iowa Governor's
STEM Advisory Council

Dr. Colburn has taken common activities used in classrooms and expertly retools them utilizing the three dimensions of the Next Generation Science Standards (NGSS) while modeling components of the 5E lesson design and making explicit connections to the Nature of Science (NOS). This book is a must read for new and experienced science educators and expands the connections and possibilities of familiar activities in the new NGSS context.

—*David Crowther, PhD*
Executive Director, Raggio Research Center for STEM Education
Professor, Science Education, University of Nevada, Reno

Learning Science by Doing Science

10 Classic Investigations Reimagined to Teach Kids How Science Really Works
Grades 3–8

Alan Colburn

A Joint Publication

CORWIN
A SAGE Publishing Company

NSTApress
National Science Teachers Association

FOR INFORMATION:

Corwin
A SAGE Company
2455 Teller Road
Thousand Oaks, California 91320
(800) 233-9936
www.corwin.com

SAGE Publications Ltd.
1 Oliver's Yard
55 City Road
London EC1Y 1SP
United Kingdom

SAGE Publications India Pvt. Ltd.
B 1/I 1 Mohan Cooperative Industrial Area
Mathura Road, New Delhi 110 044
India

SAGE Publications Asia-Pacific Pte. Ltd.
3 Church Street
#10-04 Samsung Hub
Singapore 049483

Acquisitions Editor: Erin Null
Editorial Development Manager: Julie Nemer
Editorial Assistant: Nicole Shade
Production Editor: Amy Schroller
Copy Editor: Lana Todorovic-Arndt
Typesetter: C&M Digitals (P) Ltd.
Proofreader: Dennis W. Webb
Indexer: Molly Hall
Cover and Graphic Designer: Scott Van Atta
Marketing Manager: Maura Sullivan

Printed in the United States of America

ISBN 9781506344614

This book is printed on acid-free paper.

17 18 19 20 21 10 9 8 7 6 5 4 3 2 1

Contents

Preface

I started my professional life thinking about going to medical school and becoming a doctor, so I volunteered to work in a hospital after my first year of college to learn more about the medical world. I discovered hospitals had a lot of sick people, who were understandably in bad moods. It didn't take long for my career plans to change.

I was working that summer in a hospital lab where I was supposed to look through a microscope at a large square grid showing patients' stained blood samples. It was like looking at spots on graph paper. I was supposed to randomly choose five squares and count the total number of cells I saw inside the squares. But the number I got depended on which squares I examined, as well as how I counted cells that were partway in one square and partway in another.

Although the technicians in the lab helped me with these issues, I learned that doing science was not as cut and dried as I thought from school. In my K–12 education, I'd come to see science as absolutes. The formula said F = ma, and the book said limestone fizzed when you dropped acid on it. If the numbers didn't come out the way they were supposed to, or the rock didn't fizz, I did something wrong. I screwed up somewhere.

It turned out science wasn't all objectivity and getting the right answer. Sometimes, it seemed, it was subjective. It wasn't (always) me screwing up somewhere that accounted for my "wrong answers."

In this hospital lab, I was being initiated into the way science *really* worked. And I'd like to do the same thing for you and your students.

SCIENCE CLASS THEN AND NOW

Science is coming back to elementary schools, receiving more emphasis than it has for a generation. World economics has brought renewed attention

Disciplinary core ideas are the concepts or ideas *NGSS's* authors believe everyone should know and understand; *NGSS's* content core.

Crosscutting concepts are the overarching ideas shaping the worldview or framework *NGSS's* authors believe scientists use when understanding the natural world.

Science and engineering practices are the behaviors and understandings *NGSS's* authors believe scientists and engineers use when investigating the natural world and solving problems; essentially the cognitive processes scientists and engineers use when doing science and engineering.

to science, technology, engineering, and mathematics; STEM seems to be everywhere. More and more states are including science as a part of their K–8 testing score cards. And, most important of all, new standards are sweeping the nation. One by one, little by little, states are adopting the *Next Generation Science Standards* (NGSS) or similar standards as their own. If you are reading this, there's a good chance you teach in one of those states. This book is about the kind of science envisioned by documents like NGSS. It is about helping students understand what the nature of science is, how it works, and how they can practice it the way the scientists do.

This means that the elementary or middle school science classroom can be really different from the cookbook labs and round-robin textbook reading that science classes have commonly looked like for decades. The NGSS vision is different from the one I was raised with. Maybe it's different from the one you were raised with, too. You're familiar with what we often call a cookbook activity if you have ever experienced a science lab where you followed a series of predetermined steps (like the steps in a recipe), filling in a premade table, wondering whether you got the "right answer." Someone else told you what to investigate, how to do it, what to pay attention to along the way, and what you were supposed to have learned. Someone else, in other words, did all the thinking.

NGSS, on the other hand, is built around science instruction that's always about students exploring and explaining the world around them, using a combination of specific and general ideas combined with underlying mental processes. The *NGSS* authors call the specific ideas *disciplinary core ideas* and the more general ideas *crosscutting concepts*.

The intertwined mental processes are *science and engineering practices*. I discuss NGSS more in Appendix A for readers unfamiliar with it.

The eight science and engineering practices describe what scientists do; the eight understandings about the nature of science describe characteristics of the knowledge that results. A classroom with students exploring and explaining, using SEPs, is almost certainly also a classroom where students are illustrating key tenets about the nature of science. In a real sense, it's a classroom where students are *doing* science.

SCIENCE AND ENGINEERING PRACTICES

NGSS identifies eight science and engineering practices (or SEPs). One or more of the SEPs are built into *every* performance expectation:

1. Asking Questions (for science) and Defining Problems (for engineering)

2. Developing and Using Models

3. Planning and Carrying Out Investigations

4. Analyzing and Interpreting Data

5. Using Mathematics and Computational Thinking

6. Constructing Explanations (for science) and Designing Solutions (for engineering)

7. Engaging in Argument From Evidence

8. Obtaining, Evaluating, and Communicating Information

THE NATURE OF SCIENCE

The Standards' Appendix H outlines eight understandings related to the nature of science that should be a part of all science classes, K–12:

1. Scientific investigations use a variety of methods.

2. Scientific knowledge is based on empirical evidence.

3. Scientific knowledge is open to revision in light of new evidence.

4. Science models, laws, mechanisms, and theories explain natural phenomena.

5. Science is a way of knowing.

6. Scientific knowledge assumes an order and consistency in natural systems.

7. Science is a human endeavour.

8. Science addresses questions about the natural and material world.

WHY YOU NEED THIS BOOK

In the years that followed that summer hospital experience, I studied science, worked in science labs, taught high school, and eventually became a college professor. I learned that most elementary school teachers don't like, feel comfortable with, or feel successful in science. Many are afraid of it. That's not surprising. Most people feel the same way. As one who teaches children you may have added concerns: What if something blows up? What if it gets really noisy and I lose control of the classroom? What if a kid asks me something I don't know?! These are legitimate feelings and concerns.

These worries may keep you from teaching science, or turn science into reading lessons about the natural world. Maybe, through the years, you have grown comfortable teaching a handful of science topics, a few set procedures you feel comfortable doing with your students year after year—but that's all. Or maybe science is a hands-on adventure in your classroom, with students exploring the world around them every day, all year long.

Regardless of where you fall in this spectrum, if you are reading this book, you know science is important and undoubtedly recognize the times they are a-changin' (and you recognize Bob Dylan lyrics). You care enough to put the time in to read a book about science teaching, and you have the desire to teach science effectively. For that I thank you.

You are probably less familiar with the NGSS science and engineering practices than their entwined content ideas. That's because science has often been taught as if it was nothing *but* content ideas—we're taught the conclusions, with little context for understanding where the ideas came from or how anyone figured this stuff out. However, science and engineering practices, when applied to data—our observations about the natural world—are ultimately the source of all scientific knowledge. And that's what this book is about: science and engineering practices, the nature of scientific knowledge, and how to help your students understand these the way real scientists do. There's an added payoff: When students are engaged in the kinds of hands-on, open-ended investigation activities I describe, they learn and apply science and engineering practices as a means toward learning science ideas. They learn science by doing science.

If you are implementing NGSS or other similar state science standards in your classroom, and you want to understand what you're doing, you *must* understand what's in this book. You really do.

Nothing about scientific knowledge and where it comes from makes sense except in the light of clear, convincing thinking about data. Science and engineering practices are about asking questions, collecting data to figure out answers and explanations (sometimes with help from mathematics, computers, and models), and ultimately convincing others the answers and explanations are valid. NGSS envisions your classroom as a place students are learning science by exploring and explaining.

Key Takeaway

Nothing about scientific knowledge and where it comes from makes sense except in the light of clear, convincing thinking about data.

I recognize this may sound a little scary if you've always felt uncomfortable around science. But fear not. I'll illustrate ideas with classroom activities you can relate to and give examples based on real scientists and their work. You can try the activities with your students. Most of the investigation activities I've chosen are classics that teachers have been implementing successfully for generations. That means they are tried and true, you may be able to find other teachers familiar with the activities, and you can find lots of additional guidance and resources. The best way to learn science is to do science, and doing science works better if you understand how science works. That's what I'm going to show you.

HOW TO USE THIS BOOK

You will get the most from this book if you read it in order, chapter by chapter. It's not a strict requirement, but some of the ideas in later chapters build on earlier ones. I tried to write as succinctly as possible so reading the whole book would not be burdensome.

Each chapter discusses at least one investigation activity appropriate to the 3–8 level that you could teach in your classroom. The activities are hands-on examples of ideas I discuss in the same chapter. Even when I mention particular grade levels, the investigations are almost universally appropriate across the Grades 3–8 spectrum; in some cases, I discuss how they might be taught differently in elementary and middle school. So, even if you decide not to teach an activity right away, or it seems to be aimed at grade levels other than yours, it still provides an example or application of an important idea related to the nature of scientific knowledge. Beside the practical application, and chance to introduce you to an investigation activity you might not be familiar with, I figure classroom examples might feel closer to your experiences as teachers than stories of scientists in their labs.

Each chapter is organized similarly, with common features to make this book easier for you to work with. These features include:

> *Try It!* These are step-by-step directions for a classroom investigation activity. Activities are presented as succinct plans for easy reference, including not only directions, but also necessary materials, NGSS connections, and other useful information, usually followed by a brief description of how the investigation activity fits with one or more aspects of the 5E or learning-cycle model of instruction.
>
> I try to include enough detail for you to be successful, without inundating you with too much information or slighting your teaching skills with details about nonscience teaching related classroom management. Although I provide some guidance about grade level appropriateness, you know your students and their abilities; I do not. So take my guidance

with a grain of salt, and use your own judgment about what's more and less appropriate for your kids.

Teaching Tips provide hints, suggestions, tips and other supporting ideas to deepen your understanding and readiness to execute one or more of an activity's steps. One of the really nice things about discussing time-tested activities is how easily you can find more information online related to an activity, if you feel the need for it. But I provide a couple of starting places for most of them.

What's Going On in the Science? provides additional information about the science content ideas being illustrated and developed within an investigation. This book is about science and engineering practices, and the nature of scientific knowledge, but there's no such thing as a content-free activity. This section provides a little background.

Practices in Practice sections discuss connections between an investigation activity and one or more of NGSS's science and engineering practices. Most of these sections also include a slightly more extended discussion about one or more of the practices, including information contrasting expectations for students in Grades 3–5 compared to those in Grades 6–8.

Connecting to the Nature of Science sections discuss connections with specific aspects of the nature of science illustrated in the activity. The conception of science and science's methods that students often get in school and even the larger society is somewhat inaccurate. Real science is richer, more creative, more human, and I think ultimately much more interesting than how it's often portrayed.

But wait, there's more! A third of the chapters include **Case in Point** case studies of real scientists, further illustrating how science works in real life, as well as some of the human aspects of science difficult to illustrate with classroom activities. They are written with language simple enough that you might feel comfortable sharing them with your students.

In addition, I'd like to draw your attention to the *appendices*. Appendix A provides a brief overview for readers completely unfamiliar with NGSS. I'm not assuming anything beyond the most basic familiarity with these standards, and always provide greater discussion whenever writing about parts of the document you're more likely to be unfamiliar with—its appendices, as well as the National Research Council's *Framework for K–12 Science Education: Practices, Crosscutting Concepts, and Core Ideas,* the foundation document to NGSS. I usually refer to it simply as the *Science Framework.*

Whatever I have to offer, I recognize teachers prefer guidance from their peers more than anyone else. I do, too. So for Appendix B I talked with several of my colleagues with extensive experience teaching at the elementary and middle levels to get their specific suggestions about teaching hands-on open-ended science activities. They offer advice you don't want to miss.

In the pages to come, I'll show you how ideas about the nature of science, and science and engineering practices connect to science *and* the classroom. Together we will make sure you can show your students, and have them experience for themselves, how clear thinking about data leads scientists—and students—to new ideas.

It's not scary. It's fun. If you've never seen how excited kids can get when engaged in hands-on, inquiry-based science, you are in for a treat. You can do this. I know you can do this. So let's get started!

Acknowledgments

Writing a book is an interesting experience. On one hand, it's a solitary activity. You sit in a room and write, by yourself. But on the other hand, lots of other people are involved. Without them, this book wouldn't be nearly as good as it is. My science colleagues Lora Stevens, Galen Pickett, and Christine Whitcraft graciously let me interview them, providing insights into how cutting-edge scientific research works. Josh Chesler provided information about graphical data display in elementary and middle school classrooms. Jill Grace, Marissa Stillitano, Amy Argento, and Susan Gomez-Zwiep shared their extensive elementary and middle school science teaching experiences, helping a college professor look like he understands teaching in today's classrooms.

Thomas Anderson (www.thomasanderson.net) created the book's illustrations. I think he did a great job.

My editor at Corwin, Erin Null, has been with me throughout the project. She's been instrumental in guiding the work to what you hold in your hands. The book is much better thanks to her tireless and professional efforts.

I started my teaching career in 1986. Through the years I've taught most of this book's activities to many students, most of whom are now experienced teachers themselves. Throughout the book, I stress the importance of relevant concrete background experience toward learning. Teaching these students has been *my* relevant concrete experience.

Finally, I want to recognize my wife Laura. She's been nothing but supportive, even when I was racing to meet writing deadlines, barely able to think about anything else. I am grateful for her support and guidance. Thank you, sweetie pie. You are so the one.

PUBLISHER'S ACKNOWLEDGMENTS

Corwin would like to thank the following individuals for their editorial insight and guidance:

Deanna Brunlinger
NBCT Science Teacher,
Science Department Chair
Elkhorn Area High School
Elkhorn, WI

Rosario Canizales, PhD
Science Lead Teacher
Irene C. Hernandez
Middle School
Chicago, IL

Mandy Frantti
Teacher
Munising Public Schools
Munising, MI

Dr. Rita Hagevik
University of North
Carolina at Pembroke
Graduate Director of
Science Education,
Associate Professor
Pembroke, NC

Linda Keteyian
Teacher
Detroit Public Schools
Detroit, MI

Olayinka Mohorn-Mintah
Science Teacher, 9–12
Chicago Public Schools
Chicago, IL

Christine Ruder
Teacher
Truman Elementary School
Rolla, MO

Tom Shiland
Chemistry Teacher
Saratoga Springs High School
Saratoga Springs, NY

Tony Willits
Raymond Park Middle School
Eighth Grade Science Teacher
Indianapolis, IN

About the Author

Dr. Alan Colburn is Professor of Science Education at California State University Long Beach, where he has been a faculty member since 1995. Recipient of CSULB's Distinguished Faculty Teaching Award, he holds a PhD in Science Education, an MS and BS in Biology, and a science teaching credential. Dr. Colburn has written and presented extensively during his career, including a previous book, monthly column in The Science Teacher magazine, and sections about instructional models, the 5E model of instruction, and the nature of science in California's Science Curriculum Framework.

*To all the students I've taught in the
last 30 years, and all those still to come.
Thank you for the meaning you've given my life.*

Chapter 1

Take Us Out, Mr. Data

*What's the most important thing
to know about scientific knowledge?*

In this section, you will come to see how

- scientific knowledge is based on empirical evidence, and
- science is limited to answering questions about the natural and material world.

You will be able to

- help your students perform scientific investigations via operational questions, and
- discuss similarities between student investigation activities and scientists' activities.

Here's a riddle: What do love, wind, luxury, and science all have in common? They are all easy to recognize, but hard to define, especially in ways everyone would agree upon. In the case of science, we often define the term with vague phrases, saying "science is a way of knowing" or talking about science as "a process." Sometimes my students speak even more broadly, writing that "science is everywhere" or "everything is science." Not very useful.

The demarcation problem is the philosophical issue of determining what is and is not science.

But defining science more specifically is hard. In 1997, Brian Alters published an article providing evidence that even people who study the nature of science disagreed about what it was they were studying. My colleagues quickly responded (Clough, 2007; Smith et al., 1997), accenting the disagreements as minor points. Despite widespread agreement on most points, philosophers of science nevertheless discuss the issue so much they have a special phrase to describe it: *the demarcation problem.* How do we demarcate, or distinguish, what is science from what is not?

This is a book for teachers, so let's start addressing the question via a classroom activity, a fun one I'll call Milk Fireworks. You may also recognize it by another name like "Cat's Meow," or "Breaking the Tension" (Bergman & Olson, 2011).

ACTIVITY 1

Milk Fireworks

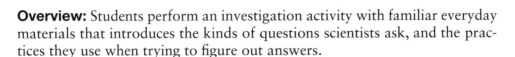

Overview: Students perform an investigation activity with familiar everyday materials that introduces the kinds of questions scientists ask, and the practices they use when trying to figure out answers.

Grades: This investigation activity is definitely appropriate for all grade levels. Older students, however, may be more successful than younger ones at coming up with their own questions and procedures to investigate.

Time needed: Part I takes less than 10 minutes, once materials are assembled. Time for the rest of the investigation activity varies, depending on teacher and student interest.

MATERIALS

Part I

- Petri dishes or similar shallow dishes
- Whole milk
- Food coloring (at least two colors)
- Toothpicks
- Liquid dish soap

Part II

- Optional additional materials: different kinds of milk (whole milk, 2% fat milk, skim milk, cream, nondairy milks), different sized and shaped containers, other liquids (e.g., water, vegetable oil, or corn syrup), other liquid detergents or dish soaps, various colors of food coloring, milk at different temperatures, and various other materials based on student and teacher interest

TEACHER INSTRUCTIONS

Part I

1. Have students take a Petri plate or other shallow dish and put a little whole milk into the dish, enough to cover the surface of the plate.

2. Have students place two drops of food coloring at the 12 o'clock and 6 o'clock positions of the dish.

3. Then have students place two drops of a different color food coloring at the 3 and 9 o'clock positions.

FIGURE 1.1 Milk Fireworks

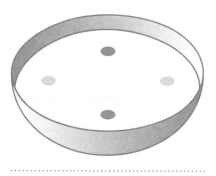

Milk Fireworks initial setup

4. Students should dip a toothpick into the milk in the center of the dish and quickly pull it out of the milk, then record their observations.

5. Now, they repeat the toothpick procedure, but first dip the end of the toothpick into dish soap.

Part II

6. Have a whole-class discussion asking students to brainstorm a list of questions they have about what's going on, recording the list of questions for everyone to see.

7. Take the list of questions students brainstormed and divide them into questions that can and cannot be answered directly by doing investigations. Accent how science is about asking and trying to answer the latter category, questions that are testable.

8. With your guidance, students can select one or more testable questions, figure out procedures to address the question, and go on to do the investigations. You'll probably want students to write the question(s) they are testing, what they did to try answering the question, and what they found. You can do this with a worksheet students fill out, journal, interactive notebook, or any other method you like.

9. After completing their investigations, students share what they found, stressing the evidence supporting their ideas (i.e., what they observed during their investigations). The sharing can be individually (through writing), via pairs or small-group discussions, via a whole-group discussion, or again, any other method you like.

What's Happening? Water tends to stick to itself, a phenomena scientists call surface tension. They believe detergents disrupt surface tension, ultimately pulling the water's surface in various directions.

TRY IT!

Unless you're teaching students about surface tension, properties of water, or colloids (see the *What's Going On in the Science* section, below), it may be difficult to connect this investigation activity with a larger 5E or learning-cycle model based science unit. However, students find the activity highly *engaging*, and it works well as an *exploration*. When you add in the fact its materials are familiar and readily available, Milk Fireworks works well early in the school year or as a 1-day standalone activity. It's easy, cool, and accents how science is about asking and answering questions.

TEACHING TIPS

Steps 1–4: Even though I don't want to spoil the spirit of inquiry, I am going to give it away: After completing the first four steps in the investigation, that is, when students dip a toothpick into the center of the milk-filled dish, they will observe nothing. Nothing much happens. But . . .

Step 5: When students then dip a toothpick with detergent on the end into the dish, something cool happens. The milk and food coloring will appear to move, with the colors swirling.

If you've never done this activity before, you should give it a try first on your own. Notice what happens, imagine how your students will react, and think through how you'll manage the activity. As you are an experienced teacher, I don't feel it's my place to tell you how to manage the more general aspects of investigation activities. But, I do offer suggestions from some of your colleagues in Appendix B.

Steps 6–8: At this stage of the activity, as you facilitate a classroom discussion about your students' observations and questions, here are three things to keep in mind.

First, I recommend you simply accept what students say, neither praising nor rejecting—by saying things like "OK," "got it," repeating what the student says, or saying "thank you"—write their questions someplace for everyone to see, and encourage continued question generation. Students will start generating questions like

> **Key Takeaway**
>
> Accepting student responses, and waiting several seconds after a student has responded, encourages other students to respond.

- "Why did the milk swirl?"
- "Will it still swirl with skim milk instead of whole milk?"
- "Will we be able to see the milk swirling without any food coloring?"
- "What will happen if we put the soap on the food coloring?"
- "Will it work with other soaps?"
- "What if we use warm milk?"

Second, once your students have generated some questions, divide them into two categories: those that can and those that cannot be answered directly via an investigation. All the questions I just listed except the first one are *operational questions*, meaning they can be investigated and answered pretty directly with evidence from investigations. To find out if the milk swirls any differently with skim and whole milk, for example, you would perform the procedure with whole milk, then perform it again keeping everything the same other than substituting in skim milk, and observe what happens. You might do it again or make sure others get the same results when they perform the same procedure, just to be sure, and you'll have an answer.

"Why did the milk swirl?" is different. It cannot be answered as directly as the others via an investigation. It's not an operational question.

If you can envision, almost immediately, how to figure out an answer to a question a student generated in Step 6, you'll know it's an operational question. "Will we be able to see the milk swirling without any food coloring?" Repeat the procedure as before, but don't use any food coloring this time. "What will happen if we put soap directly on the food coloring?" Repeat the procedure as before, but put the soap directly on the food coloring this time.

Operational questions like these, sometimes also called *investigable questions*, have special significance for elementary and middle school teachers. The more directly investigable a question, the closer the idea being investigated comes to being tangible and directly observable. And the more tangible an idea, the more likely students are to understand it. Generally speaking, elementary and middle school students are more likely to understand concrete, tangible, observable ideas than more abstract ones. Tangible concepts are more likely to be near students' experiences than abstract concepts. Directly investigable questions and problems don't just make for good science, as I explain below, they also make for good learning.

Third, even after limiting the list to operational questions, some questions may not reasonably be addressed in the classroom setting. They may be too complex, take too much time, or use materials you don't have. You may need to help students eliminate questions they cannot reasonably complete in Step 8, even if the questions are investigable. Still, it's good to have a variety of materials available for the investigations students might carry out. I listed several above.

WHAT'S GOING ON IN THE SCIENCE?

The scientifically accepted explanation for the swirling milk behavior seen in Milk Fireworks is surprisingly complex. That's why I didn't link it to a specific *Next Generation Science Standards* (NGSS) disciplinary core idea (and associated performance expectation). It's often explained in terms of surface tension. Scientists would say water molecules stick to themselves (one part of the molecule has a slight positive charge, another part a slight negative charge, and the oppositely charged sides of adjacent molecules are attracted). This stickiness explains why light bugs can walk on the surface of water, and you can slightly overfill a glass without spilling. Soaps and detergents chemically break surface tension. When the surface tension is broken, water molecules start moving around, and we see the food coloring being carried along with the moving water.

This explanation is fairly satisfying and, as such, can be used to tie the investigation activity in with content about the structure and properties of matter (which is disciplinary core idea PS1-A, encompassed in NGSS performance expectations like 5-PS1-1, "Develop a model to describe that matter is made of particles too small to be seen.").

However, the explanation falls short a little. You can demonstrate this empirically by repeating the procedure, but substituting water for milk. If food coloring moves (only) because water's surface tension is broken, you'd predict similar observations with water as for milk. I'll let you test for yourself to see what happens. That's the kind of person I am.

A better explanation is beyond the scope of this book. However, milk is a special type of solution (a colloid). Fats and other substances are suspended in water. Ultimately, the soap probably not only breaks the surface tension, but also literally connects the water and fats in the milk in ways that disrupt their previous connection. Part of the movement, we observe comes from the effects of this change, too.

PRACTICES IN PRACTICE

As I mentioned in the preface, in Appendix F NGSS's authors describe the activity of science in terms of eight overarching science and engineering practices (SEPs). One or more of these practices are part of *every* NGSS performance expectation, and they represent what scientists do when creating new knowledge. (Performance expectations are NGSS's equivalent of standards. Readers can find a brief introduction to NGSS in Appendix A.)

Just about any time students complete investigations as open ended as the ones in this activity, they will be using multiple practices. That's how it should be. If you select an investigation activity to teach your class, see if you can identify more than one SEP students use during the activity. It should be possible to do this with classroom activities in which students are learning science by doing science. In fact, I'd suggest being careful before selecting any classroom activity where students are only using a single SEP; strive for activities where students use multiple SEPs. NGSS's authors stress this point on p. 3 of Appendix F with boldface type: "The eight practices are not separate; they intentionally overlap and interconnect." Let's examine some of the ways this plays out in this investigation activity:

- Students are clearly *asking questions or defining problems (SEP1)* in Milk Fireworks. After all, the activity's main goal is helping students recognize investigable questions. As an elementary or middle school teacher, you might not be teaching students about phrases like "empirical evidence," but students can still understand that scientists ask and answer questions answerable with observations and data. To be most effective, the teacher should be explicit in making sure students recognize and learn the activity's purpose.

- Students are *planning and carrying out investigations (SEP3)* in Step 8 of Part II above. After choosing an operational question to investigate, students go on to complete the investigation. As teacher, you can increase the likelihood students learn about how science works by telling them scientists answer questions by planning and carrying out investigations. You can also encourage students to write a description of what they plan to do, an important part of planning and carrying out investigations (so that scientists can later compare their procedures and results, especially if others thought they were answering the same question but obtained different results; comparing procedures it usually turns out they actually performed slightly different procedures that can account for the different results).

- Once students finish their investigations, they will immediately, almost instinctively, *analyze and interpret data (SEP4)* when deciding on answers to their questions. As a teacher, you can explicitly point out that they are interpreting what they observed to come up with their conclusions (perhaps by simply teaching students and then using the phrase "interpreting data" whenever appropriate), adding that scientists do the same thing—they always base their thoughts on data.

CONNECTING TO THE NATURE OF SCIENCE

Our natural human tendency when we observe something interesting or unexpected is to immediately ask, "Why?" We want to explain our observations. We witness *phenomena* and try to make sense of what we have observed. My colleague Jill Grace defines phenomena as things in the natural world that can be observed and wondered about. Given this definition, empirical data would be firsthand observations about phenomena.

Phenomena are things in the natural world that can we can observe and wonder about.

In its simplest sense, this is the essence of how science works—observe phenomena you find interesting, for whatever reasons; notice patterns, trends, regularities; try to explain or make sense of what you've observed. In the Milk Fireworks investigation activity, the swirling milk is unexpected and therefore interesting. Students are naturally curious about what's going on (so are adults!), and further experiments help them understand and make sense. **In the Milk Fireworks investigation activity, students are *doing* science.** They are asking scientific questions and carrying out investigations. Their findings are scientific knowledge. I grant that "My food coloring swirls better with whole milk than skim milk" may not win the Nobel Prize but it *is* scientific knowledge!

> ### Key Takeaway
> Science is a way of making sense of our observations as we witness particular phenomena

NGSS discusses eight major themes related to the nature of science that should be part of schooling at all levels, K–12. I listed them in the preface and Appendix A of this book. They are discussed more fully in the NGSS Appendix H (NGSS Lead States, 2013b).

I believe the best place to start examining these themes is recognizing that scientific knowledge must ultimately be based on evidence from observations. There has to be some sort of physical evidence supporting an idea if it counts as science. One of the NGSS Appendix H themes is "scientific knowledge is based on empirical evidence," and another is "science is limited to answering questions about the natural and material world" (NGSS Lead States, 2013b). I've mentioned empirical evidence a few times already. *Empirical evidence* is the kind of evidence that comes from the senses, the observations we make by seeing, smelling, listening, etc. If phenomena are things in the natural world that can we can observe and wonder about, empirical data are firsthand observations about phenomena.

Empirical evidence is the kind of evidence that comes from the senses—seeing, smelling, listening, etc.; often referred to as synonymous with data.

How do these themes relate to Milk Fireworks? When students doing Part II of the investigation come up with answers to their operational questions, the knowledge they create is based on empirical evidence—what they observe while doing their investigations. They are demonstrating one of the key tenets about the nature of scientific knowledge: Answers to science questions are based on empirical evidence.

The other theme, "science is limited to answering questions about the natural and material world," relates to Milk Fireworks in that operational questions, by definition, will be questions about the natural and material world (note that the opposite of natural is supernatural; it's not "artificial"). If student questions include examples like "Why do we have to do this?", "Does this count for a grade?", or "Do you like teaching science?" then they would *not* be scientific questions. They are not about the observable world, and they cannot be answered with evidence from observations. Many valuable and important questions are nevertheless not scientific questions.

To help you think about what your students might be able to understand about these themes, NGSS Appendix H differentiates expectations or standards for Grade 3–5 and 6–8 students.

- **In the 3–5 Classroom:** NGSS Appendix H notes learning outcomes and expectations students in these grade levels should ultimately understand include
  - science findings are limited to what can be answered with empirical evidence;
  - science findings are based on recognizing patterns; and
  - scientists use tools and technologies to make accurate measurements and observations.

- **In the 6–8 Classroom:** On the other hand, the appendix notes learning outcomes and expectations students in these grade levels should ultimately understand include
  - scientific knowledge is constrained by human capacity, technology, and materials;
  - science limits its explanations to systems that lend themselves to observation and empirical evidence;
  - science knowledge can describe consequences of actions, but is not responsible for society's decisions;
  - science knowledge is based upon logical and conceptual connections between evidence and explanations; and
  - science disciplines share common rules of obtaining and evaluating empirical evidence.

Beside their use as guideposts for what your students might or might not be able to understand, these expectations can also provide middle school teachers with a teaching progression. If you are a middle school teacher, look first to Grade 3–5 expectations and decide whether you believe your students understand them. If not, start there. Worry about Grade 6–8 expectations only after you believe most students understand Grade 3–5 expectations.

Case in Point

The Story of Barbara McClintock

Nobel Prize–winning scientist Barbara McClintock

To end the Chapter, I present the story of Barbara McClintock's work. Perhaps you can use it to illustrate for your students some aspects of what science is and how it works. Or perhaps you'll just use it yourself toward that goal. At the end of the story, I'll discuss some ways her story is similar to your students making food coloring swirl!

Barbara McClintock and modern genetics were born together, around the turn of the 20th century. Geneticists in the 1920s were trying to link how things looked (or behaved) with parts of their chromosomes. McClintock became fascinated by corn whose kernels had yellow and purple spots (kernels are usually either all yellow or all purple).

Just as students see food coloring swirling in a dish and wonder what's going on, McClintock saw funny looking corn and wondered what was going on. Recognizing a pattern, like the occasional presence of spotted corn kernels, however, is different than an explanation or model that helps us understand and predict the corn's behavior.

McClintock *really* wanted to understand what was going on. She moved next to her corn field and worked for years, by herself, experimenting, collecting, and analyzing data.

To explain her observations, she came to suspect something was breaking in a particular chromosome. She reasoned if the area (or gene) on the chromosome she studied was working properly, the resulting corn kernel would look purple. And if it was not working properly, the kernel would look yellow or white. She came to the creative conclusion that something in the middle of the area (or gene) was appearing and disappearing, turning it off and on.

Scientists at the time had a model of a chromosome as being like a string. A gene was a piece of the string. Every chromosome, they believed, consisted of many genes arranged in a sequence, one after another like pearls on a necklace. No one thought about chromosomes or genes changing the way McClintock did. She thought very differently than others about the chromosome model.

Year after year, McClintock amassed overwhelming data supporting her idea. But nothing is considered "true" in science unless it has been accepted by peers. And so, 6 years after beginning the work, she felt ready to stand before her colleagues and tell them about her work.

At a 1951 symposium before a group of leading scientists, she laid out evidence supporting her model. And then she waited to see how her colleagues would react. The work would mean little unless she convinced other scientists of its merit.

And she did not get it.

She went on to publish the work in a long paper. And almost no one read the article.

How would you react if you spent 6 years working on something, and no one paid attention? If your peers didn't seem to care? I'd be mortified, crushed.

"I was startled when I found they didn't understand it, didn't take it seriously," McClintock said,

> but it didn't bother me. I just knew I was right. People get the idea that your ego gets in the way a lot of time—ego in the sense of wanting returns. But you don't care about those returns. You have the enormous pleasure of working on it. The returns are not what you're after. (McGrayne, 1993, p. 168)

Wow. That is one dedicated scientist!

Although she had no idea it would happen, the rest of the scientific world finally started catching up to McClintock when the same thing was observed in things other than corn. The scientific understanding of genes, like all scientific knowledge, started to change as evidence continued rolling in supporting McClintock's ideas. Honors started rolling in and, in 1983—32 years after her initial presentation—Barbara McClintock was awarded the Nobel Prize.

Remarkably, she seemed to harbor no bitterness in the time it took for the rest of the scientific community to come to accept her work. Thirty-two years is a long time, but she was emphatic about the point. "It's such a pleasure to carry out an experiment when you think of something—carry it out and watch it go—it's a great, great pleasure," she said.

> It couldn't be nicer. . . . I just have been so interested in what I was doing, and it's been such a pleasure, such a deep pleasure, that I never thought of stopping. . . . I've had such a good time, I can't imagine having a better one. . . . I've had a very, very satisfying and interesting life. (McGrayne, 1993, p. 173)

CONCLUSION

This chapter and much of this book is about you and ultimately your students understanding what's unique about science as a way of knowing. (I didn't mention it previously, but the idea *science is a way of knowing*—which implies there are other ways of knowing—is one of NGSS's nature of science themes.) This chapter is also about two other themes—that *science addresses questions about the observable world*, using *knowledge based on empirical evidence*. Barbara McClintock was studying questions about the observable world, creating answers matching the available empirical evidence, and so are your students when investigating swirling milk.

The McClintock story illustrates how models and explanations are different from the observations themselves. I did not emphasize the point discussing the Milk Fireworks activity investigation—it's for you, understanding the ideas at a deeper level than your students—but your students' investigations in the activity help them understand what's happening with the phenomena *without necessarily developing scientific models explaining why the swirling occurred*. But that does *not* mean the investigation isn't appropriate for young children.

Finally, McClintock's work demonstrates the human side of science. Science is a social activity, requiring scientists convince each other their ideas work. Children engaged in Milk Fireworks will exhibit their own human tendencies and, undoubtedly, will also try convincing each other their ideas work. Sometimes we forget the human side of science. An accurate representation of science should always include our human-ness. The next chapter builds on this one, as we discuss important knowledge and questions that are *not* scientific.

Additional Resources

To learn more about Milk Fireworks, see Bergman, D. J., & Olson, J. (2011). Got inquiry? *Science and Children*, 48(7), 44–48. You can also see the basic procedure illustrated on Steve Spangler's science website at www.stevespanglerscience.com/lab/experiments/milk-color-explosion/. His version differs from mine only in where food coloring is initially placed. Try both versions; see which one you like better!

Chapter 2

Think Different

How is scientific thinking different from everyday thinking?

In this section, you will come to see how

- science is different from everyday, commonsense thinking; and
- mental models are often important to scientific explanations.

You will be able to

- challenge your students' mental models with the 5E or learning-cycle model of instruction.

NGSS's authors describe science as "a way of knowing," which implies *other* ways of knowing must exist. Understanding the differences between science and other ways of knowing helps us clarify what science is and is not. All sorts of vital questions we consider in our lives are *not* scientific. We ask about what is right and wrong, how to behave, where and how to place our faith in a spiritual presence beyond the natural world, and what's really important in life. Our answers to these questions come from our parents, other authority figures, sacred texts, etc., but not from data or scientific investigations.

Such questions are arguably the most important ones we will ever consider— but they are not scientific questions. As NGSS points out, science is limited to addressing questions about the natural or material world. Science cannot answer every question.

To help clarify and strengthen your understanding of what science is, this chapter focuses on how scientific thinking differs from everyday, common-sense thinking. I'll also introduce the idea of conceptual change teaching— how to help students recognize the differences between their common sense and the scientifically accepted understanding of concepts.

I think these ideas are important not only for better understanding how science works, but also because students bring their own commonsense ways of understanding the world to your classroom. Understanding how common sense works helps you understand how your students' minds work.

COMMON SENSE VS. SCIENCE

Common sense describes how we *intuitively* understand the parts of the world we interact with in ways that are practical, specific, and personal. It has kept our forebears alive for hundreds of thousands of years. Common sense works for us here and now; whether it applies anywhere else or for anyone else is less important.

This distinguishes it from scientific ideas, because science searches for universal, broadly applicable truths. Science is about finding patterns and explanations that apply not only here and now, but also everywhere else, in the past and (presumably) the future. One of NGSS's understandings about the nature of science is "scientific knowledge assumes an order and consistency in natural systems." Consistency and order imply predictability, throughout time and location. (In fact, you could characterize science as being limited to investigating those parts of the observable universe we believe to be ordered and predictable.)

Key Takeaway

Science strives to find universal, broadly applicable truths.

A universe where we assume order and predictability means not only does your dropped pencil fall to the ground, but we assume dropped pencils have *always* fallen to the ground, *everywhere*.

Commonsense experiences and scientific ideas often seem at odds with one another when scientists start looking for common features they can generalize and then try to explain. Scientific thinking abstracts from individual experience. Physicists know objects in motion tend to remain in motion, but in our individual experiences, they tend to come to rest. Astronomers know the Earth revolves around a stationary sun, but in our everyday experiences, the sun rises, moves across the sky, and sets. The idea invisibly tiny organisms (germs) could cause illness and even death seemed ridiculous for many years, flying in the face of common sense, as did the idea continents move. Abstract ideas like friction, the heliocentric model of the solar system, the germ theory of disease causation, and plate tectonic theory I just alluded to all seem, at first, to differ from intuitive observations about how the world works.

Key Takeaway

Science is a human endeavor and a social activity. —NGSS Appendix H

Science tries to find ideas that work everywhere, while everyday thinking differs in concentrating on what's happening here and now. Scientific ideas must be agreed upon by a wide-ranging group of peers before being accepted—that's one of the reasons we often describe science as a social activity—while everyday commonsense ideas only need to be OK to us as individuals; it doesn't matter what other people think.

The distinction between intuitive, commonsense ways of thinking about the world and science's often abstract, unintuitive models has an added payoff for you as teachers. It's mirrored in the classroom when we think about teaching for *conceptual change*. This idea, widely accepted throughout the education community, begins by recognizing that children come to school with intuitive, preconceived models of how the world works—basically common sense—and the teacher's task is not to "give" children ideas, but to help them *replace* their commonsense ideas with ideas like those accepted by the scientific community.

Conceptual change is a model defining learning as the process of changing preconceived ideas about how the world works; usually discussed in terms of learners changing ideas, frameworks, or mental models to better align with current scientific understandings.

So let's dive in with a detailed look at a classroom example of how conceptual change teaching, science and engineering practices, and the nature of science go hand in hand: a classic activity teaching students about electrical circuits. Fittingly for purposes of NGSS, it's also an engineering problem.

Electrical Circuits

Overview: Students learn about electrical circuits while experimenting with light bulbs, batteries, and wires.

Grades: Fourth grade or higher

Time needed: 30–45 minutes for Steps 1–3; remainder of activity could last several hours, spread out over multiple days, depending on children's interests and how much the teacher extends the activity.

MATERIALS

- Flashlight bulbs
- 1.5-volt batteries
- Wire, wire strippers to create pieces of wire around 6 inches long
- Flashlight bulb holders (for Step 8)
- Knife switches (optional)

INSTRUCTIONS

1. Show students a flashlight bulb, 1.5-volt flashlight battery, and a single piece of wire. Ask students to draw in their science notebooks how they would connect the three items to make the bulb light.

2. Pass out batteries, bulbs, and wires to students and let them test their ideas by connecting the items the way they described in their models to see what happens.

3. Allow students to now explore various combinations of wire, battery, and bulb, trying to find a combination that lights the bulb.

4. Once students have figured out how to light a bulb, challenge them to see how they can (and cannot) rearrange the battery or bulb to find other combinations keeping the bulb lit. As before, have them draw pictures in their notebooks, keeping track of arrangements that do and do not light the bulbs.

5. As a whole group, ask students about arrangements that did and did not light the bulb, gathering and showing student diagrams, and dividing them into categories of those whose models made the bulb light up, and those that didn't.

6. Contrasting the two piles, explain to students how arrangements that lit bulbs have a loop—a circuit—where a path can be traced from

one end of the battery, through a wire, through the side and tip of the bulb, back to the other end of the battery. This is the place to formally introduce students to the concept of an electrical circuit and, possibly, an electrical conductor.

7. Show students diagrams or pictures of batteries, bulbs, and wires arranged various ways and asked whether they think the bulbs will light, and why.

8. Extend the challenge, asking students to figure out how to make two bulbs light.

What's Happening? Bulbs will light when a complete electrical circuit is present, a loop connecting both ends of a battery with the tips and metal casings surrounding the bulbs.

NGSS Connections: Performance expectation (PE) 4-PS3-2 says students who demonstrate understanding can make observations to provide evidence that energy can be transferred from place to place by sound, light, heat, and electric currents.

PE 4-PS3-4 says they can apply scientific ideas to design, test, and refine a device that converts energy from one form to another.

TRY IT!

I modified this lesson from more classical versions to fit the 5E model of instruction. The 5E model takes students through an inquiry-based process whose phases are typically referred to as "Engage, Explore, Explain, Elaborate, and Evaluate." "Elaboration" is also sometimes called either Expansion or Extension. I'm using the terms interchangeably. Regardless, the *5E model* (Bybee, 1997) or its parent, the *learning-cycle* model of instruction (Marek & Cavallo, 1997), helps teachers elicit, challenge, and change students' everyday ideas to better fit scientifically accepted ideas. Well known and accepted in the science education community, the model begins with two key ideas. Learning an idea is enhanced if students

1. Have first had relevant, concrete experiences with the idea (reflected in the exploratory phase of the models), and then

2. Use the new idea, in a different context, after being introduced to it (reflected in the application or expansion phases of the models).

In this investigation activity, students first essentially draw their mental model of an electrical circuit, test their thinking, and almost always find the bulb doesn't light. This surprising result *engages* their thinking. Finding various combinations of battery, bulb, and wire that *do* light a bulb, gets students *exploring*, challenging, and testing all sorts of ideas—their ideas. The *explanation* phase of the 5E model (called content introduction in the learning cycle) happens when the teacher helps students contrast arrangements that did and did not light bulb and then formally introduces the concept of an electrical circuit—an idea students have now already experienced for themselves in previous steps. Finally, as students use their new learning to predict whether various arrangements will light or trying to figure out how to make *two* bulbs light, they are applying their learning in new contexts—the *elaboration* phase of the 5E model (called application in the learning cycle). I didn't include it here, but any *evaluation* you do in the unit serves as the fifth E.

5E model is an updated version of the learning cycle model of instruction, adding explicit instructional phases for engaging students' attention and evaluating their learning; usually discussed in terms of its five instructional phases—Engage, Explore, Explain, Elaborate, Evaluate.

Learning cycle is an instructional model in which students explore ideas before being formally introduced to them, and then use their learning in new contexts afterwards; it's usually discussed in terms of exploration, content introduction, and application instructional phases.

Key Takeaway

Learning is more likely if students have had experience with an idea before they're introduced to it.

Key Takeaway

Learning is more likely if students use an idea in a new context after being introduced to it.

FIGURE 2.1 Circuits 1

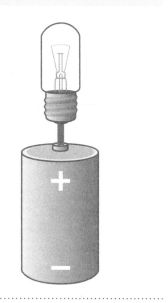

Common initial idea about lighting the bulb

TEACHING TIPS

Step 1: Children and adults often draw a diagram with a wire going from the + side of the battery to the metal tip of the bulb. Nothing is touching or connected to the − side of the battery or the metal casing on the bulb. This represents a mental model in which we explain what's happening by saying electrical energy, stored in the battery, travels through the wire and into the bulb, where it is converted to light and heat. When the energy stored in the battery is used up, the bulb no longer lights.

The model seemingly explains why we need to periodically replace batteries, why our bulbs stop producing light when they burn out, and it supports the way flashlights look when we open them up—we see a light bulb and (one or) two batteries stacked on top of each other. At first glance, the model *seems* to explain lots of home lighting, too, which often *looks like* just one wire cord connected to a light bulb socket. This is a practical model, a common-sense model that seems to fit our everyday experiences.

The key words here are *seems* and *looks like*. The problem with the model is that, when applied in this investigation activity as a basis for lighting a bulb, it doesn't work. A battery, bulb, and wire connected this way don't light. (Give it a try!)

Step 2: Thus, when students go on to test their thinking, the results often surprise them. Moreover, seeing the model diagrams students wrote before trying to make a bulb light allows you a glimpse into their everyday, common sense view of electricity and electrical circuits (especially if you also ask them to tell you about their ideas).

Step 3: You can scaffold student learning with hints provided by questions asking for predictions, like "Do you think the bulb will still light if you turn the battery around?" and "Do you think you could touch the wire to a different part of the bulb and still have it light?" Because science is empirical, hands-on, and fun, your responses to whatever students say, in each case, is not necessarily "you're right" or "you're wrong." A better response is, "OK, find out!"

Scientific knowledge is based on clear, convincing thinking about empirical data. So, as students try to figure out how to light the bulb, I recommend they record in their notebooks drawings not only of arrangements of battery, bulb, and wire that lit the bulb, but *also* arrangements where the bulb did *not* light. Unlit bulbs may not solve the original problem, but they do provide valuable information—data—which is analyzed and interpreted (SEP4) in figuring out what it takes to light a bulb. Once students start feeling like they understand what it takes to make an electrical circuit, once they start developing models (SEP2), they can return to the circuits where bulbs did not light and see whether their models explain why.

NGSS Connection:
SEP4 Analyzing and interpreting data

NGSS Connection:
SEP2 Developing and using models

After first exploring on their own to understand and recognize conditions under which bulbs will and won't light, students begin to recognize problems with their intuitive, commonsense models and (hopefully) feel the need to be introduced in some fashion to a different model explaining observations about electricity and electrical circuits. Students' (and adults') intuitive ideas have served them well enough in their lives. It's only now, when challenged to use their ideas in a larger context, that they begin to see problems.

Step 4: Once students have figured out how to light a bulb, they go on to find alternate arrangements of battery, bulb, and wire resulting in lit bulbs (like turning the battery 180 degrees, so whatever was touching the + side is now touching the – side of the battery, or trading which parts of the bulb touch the wire and battery). When most students have found at least two arrangements to light the bulb, and some have found three to four arrangements, Step 4 comes to a close.

Steps 5 and 6: The basic idea here is to gather students' results, learn about their thinking, and use that as the starting point for some sort of direct instruction, introducing the concept of electrical circuits (and maybe conductors). As a skilled teacher, you know your students well and have favorite ways to introduce concepts, so I leave the details to you. You might want to pool student diagrams of combinations that did not light a bulb and, separately, combinations that did light a bulb. You might also ask students about what's different between the two groups, or even just to share their thinking about what has to happen for a bulb to light. I am not advocating a single approach—as long as students get the chance to use what they were introduced to in Step 5.

Introducing students to the concepts—the scientific idea of an electrical circuit and, possibly conductors and insulators—will differ for younger and older children.

FIGURE 2.2 Circuits 2

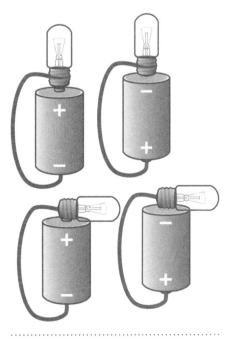

Ways to light the bulb

- **In the 3–5 classroom:** Your definition of an electrical circuit should focus on observables. An electrical circuit is essentially a metal loop or path between the battery's + and − poles. Showing or telling students about what's inside a light bulb helps illustrate the idea, especially when you trace the metal "path" leading from the light bulb's tip, through its filament, to its metal jacket outside the bulb.

- **In the 6–8 classroom:** Students can extend the 3–5 level circuit concept by doing something like using arrows to show the electrical path from one end of the battery to the other end. Your definition of an electrical circuit can be expanded to introduce a more abstract idea of electrical current, explained by a model in which electrons transmit electrical energy from the battery through the wires.

Importantly, *by the time you tell students about circuits* (regardless of grade level) *they will already have experienced the concept firsthand for themselves.* You will, essentially, be putting a label onto something they have already learned. (By the way, see how you make use of data about bulb arrangements that did *not* light? All data can ultimately prove useful. So-called negative results are still important, both to science and learning.)

Step 7: If you have access to bulb holders, this would be a good place to introduce them to your students, making sure they understand not only how to use them but also how they work.

Students should, as before, make diagrams for their notebooks. They can be challenged to make two bulbs light now, and then go on to find a *second* way to make two bulbs light. Students are continuing to expand their learning by applying it in a new context—figuring out how to use circuits to make two bulbs light followed, again, by more teacher-centered instruction introducing the concepts of series and parallel circuits. A *series circuit* consists of the battery and two bulbs connected as one big loop—the circuit goes from one end of the battery, through the first bulb, the second bulb, and then back to the other end of the battery. A *parallel circuit* is illustrated in the diagram.

FIGURE 2.3 Parallel Circuit Image

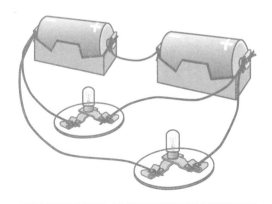

Parallel circuit

Additional activities can help students understand related concepts, from something as observable as a switch to ideas as unobservable as voltage, current, and energy conversion. (There are two ways, from an electrical standpoint, to light a pair of bulbs—a series circuit and a parallel circuit. Students can differentiate the two methods, empirically, when you tell them with one method, removing a bulb from the circuit will cause the other bulb to be *unlit*—that's the series circuit—while with the other method—the parallel circuit—removing a bulb from the circuit will have *no effect* on the second bulb.)

WHAT'S GOING ON IN THE SCIENCE?

Scientists describe electrical *currents* powered by the battery as charged particles moving in one direction (*direct current*). Their model explains how chemical reactions inside a battery provide energy that pushes charged particles out one pole of the battery, while essentially pulling them in the other pole. *Voltage* is a measure of how strongly the charged particles are being pushed out the battery. A little 9-volt battery can push charged particles more strongly than a 1.5-volt flashlight battery, even though the 9-volt battery is physically smaller (another of science's unintuitive ideas).

> **Key Takeaway**
>
> Scientific models, laws, mechanisms, and theories explain natural phenomena. —NGSS Appendix H

Scientists and engineers call materials that permit charged particles to move through easily (like metals) *conductors,* while those requiring much more effort (voltage) are called *insulators*. Scientists and engineers model conductors, like metals, as having particles that move easily. In their model, one particle more or less bumps into another, transferring energy, which then bumps into another particle, transferring the energy, and so on, and so on.

The model, however, requires a path allowing particles (electrons) to both "leave" and "enter" the battery. Sometimes a bicycle chain is used as an analogy—the energy supplied by the bicyclist is like a battery creating electrical energy, the turning wheel on the back of the bike is like a bulb using most of that energy, and the chain is like the wire transferring energy from source to destination. The chain (or wire) only allows all this to happen if it's connected in a complete loop. (This model differs from the commonsense model describing a one-way connection from the battery to the light bulb.)

The light bulb's filament gets in the way of easy, orderly energy transfer—it resists electrical current—creating heat and light energy along the way, and the wires themselves impede energy transformation a little bit, too.

Logically, the more forcefully charged particles are being pushed out a battery (i.e., the higher the voltage), the more particles should move through connected wires (i.e., the higher the current). Similarly, adding batteries to a simple circuit (increasing voltage) predicts a brighter bulb (more current to the bulb).

Electrical circuits have long been a popular elementary school science activity and high school science topic. For more information about the elementary or middle school unit and its key ideas, see the end of the chapter.

CONNECTIONS TO THE NATURE OF SCIENCE

I opened the chapter by pointing out how our everyday, intuitive ideas about how the world works—what I'm calling commonsense ideas—often differ from scientifically accepted ideas. In some ways, common sense is a natural way of thinking, and science is an unnatural way of thinking (Wolpert, 1992). Common sense is whatever works for you now; science ideas have to be acceptable to a large group of people, the scientific community. Common sense is oriented toward the present; science tries to find ideas and explanations that fit past, present, and future observations (by assuming nature behaves the same everywhere). Common sense is specific, science is generalized. To make all this happen, science often abstracts the more general features of an idea or explanation.

Hands-on, open-ended investigations (within a learning cycle or 5E lesson sequence) are great for showing students how their commonsense, intuitive ideas or models may not work in all situations—a condition many learning theorists believe necessary before true conceptual change will happen—while simultaneously helping students understand how their actions and thoughts are just like those of scientists. Open-ended activities can show students situations where their commonsense, intuitive thinking *doesn't* work, starting the kind of mental processes ("cognitive dissonance" we call it) helping students be receptive to different ideas—the more general, often more abstract ideas in scientific models.

The bridge from common sense to scientific views lies in challenging and broadening experiences. Scientists are interested in explaining and predicting as universally as possible. The more broadly or universally applicable an idea, the better, as far as science is concerned.

Toward these ends, when students connect batteries, bulbs, and wires to find out whether bulbs light, they are testing ideas to see whether evidence from observation supports them. They are doing science! You can help students make the connection via things you say throughout activities like this one:

- You can remind students how doing science is not about just reading from a book or even listening to a teacher, how it's coming up with ideas and testing them by doing investigations and collecting data.

- You can point out to students that when they connect batteries, bulbs, and wires *they* are doing investigations, just as scientists and engineers explore their ideas by doing investigations.
- When students write down in their notebooks what they did and what happened, you call it "collecting data."
- You can point out to students how their diagrams are a kind of model (especially when diagrams are accompanied by explanations of what's happening), and help them understand how their investigations are testing their models. The link is reinforced with questions like, "Tell me about the model you were using when you connected the battery, bulb, and wire. What did you think would happen to make the bulb light?"
- Because students become sensitized early to the idea that science labs have right and wrong answers, and a non-lit bulb seems like a wrong answer, I think it's important to respond with something like "I know the bulb didn't light, but your model makes a lot of sense to me." (And, I should add, there's a pretty good chance the student's model *will* make a lot of sense to you! Just because it's scientifically "wrong" doesn't mean it isn't logical, reasonable, or even sophisticated.)

> **Key Takeaway**
>
> Scientific investigations use a variety of methods. —NGSS Appendix H

> **Key Takeaway**
>
> Scientific models, laws, mechanisms, and theories explain natural phenomena. —NGSS Appendix H

PRACTICES IN PRACTICE

The ideas we tend to retain are those we create for ourselves. And when students do investigations where they create ideas for themselves, they are almost certainly going to be making use of multiple science and engineering practices. *Doing* science is a powerful way to *learn* science. As with every investigation activity in this book, students use multiple science and engineering practices (SEPs) in this chapter's activity.

> **Key Takeaway**
>
> The ideas we tend to retain are those we create for ourselves.

> **NGSS Connection:**
> SEP1 Asking questions or defining problems

- Students are *asking questions or defining problems* (SEP1) when trying to make a light bulb light.
- Students are *planning and carrying out an investigation* (SEP3) whenever they connect their batteries, bulbs, and wires together, testing their ideas about electrical circuits.

> **NGSS Connection:**
> SEP3 Planning and carrying out investigations

- Students are *analyzing and interpreting data* (SEP4) when they observe whether the bulb lights.
- Students are *obtaining, evaluating, and communicating information* (SEP8) when they talk together and share notebook observations, and *engaging in argument from evidence* (SEP7) if they try to convince each other their ideas are "right."

Perhaps most significantly for my discussion this chapter, this investigation is illustrating SEP2 *developing and using models.*

NGSS's Appendix F distinguishes grade level expectations for abilities using SEP2.

- **In Grades 3–5:** Students can test models and identify their limitations (which they do, for example, when discovering their electrical circuit model does not accurately predict how to make a bulb light). Sometimes students in these grade spans have difficulty conceiving of a model as anything other than a bigger or smaller duplication of observable reality (like a model of a car as a small version of a "real" car).

- **In Grades 6–8:** Students can test models and identify their limitations, like students in Grades 3–5, but older students are expected to become more sophisticated in their abilities. Students in this age range can usually begin creating and testing models whose mechanisms or factors are more abstract and unobservable than those of younger students. Where younger students may see models as duplications of observable reality, older students can begin moving away from the idea models are limited to copies and move toward models as more abstracted representations whose value lies in how well they predict and/or explain. A map, for example, is an accurate model for predicting and understanding how to travel between places, even when it leaves out observable features of the land. Models of highway traffic flow are even more highly abstracted; they are series of equations predicting average traffic speeds given various variable conditions. (So models describing or explaining concepts like electrical current or voltage are more likely to be understandable to older than younger children.)

Science education researchers have extensively examined students' models—what I'm calling intuitive or commonsense models—about electricity and electrical circuits (Osborne & Freyberg, 1985; Shipstone, 1985). Three models (used to explain how a battery lights a bulb) are particularly common; each differs from the scientifically accepted model:

- A model in which "electricity" or "current" leaves one end of a battery, moves through a wire, enters the bulb, and turns into light and heat. I've discussed this *unipolar* model throughout the chapter.

- A model in which electricity or current leaves both the + and − poles of the battery and meets inside the bulb, where something like electrical charges essentially collide and destroy each other, creating light and heat.

- A model in which electrical current leaves one pole of the battery and gets used up as it makes its way around the circuit, sort of like a runner who's filled with energy at the beginning of a race, but moving much more slowly by the time he or she limps over the finish line.

This chapter has centered on challenging student ideas about the unipolar model. Students in Grades 3–5 can test it, see its problems, be ready for alternatives, and begin developing models where circuits are conceived of as "loops" or "paths" of conducting material going between battery poles. In addition, sometimes students whose electrical models involve charges colliding with each other do not believe it's possible to light a bulb with just one wire; this model, too, is challenged when a bulb is seen to be lit by a battery and single wire.

Although the colliding-charges and current-gets-used-up models might be challenged by carefully noting how bulbs in various types of circuits do or do not dim as additional bulbs are added, the models involve unobservable ideas, and replacing them with scientifically more accepted models may be more challenging until students are in Grades 6–8 or, sometimes, even older.

CONCLUSION

There are similarities in the way students learn science and scientists do science. When NGSS says "scientific knowledge is open to revision in light of new evidence," that means scientific knowledge changes, old ideas are replaced by new ones. And when it says "scientific knowledge is based on empirical evidence," that means the changes are supposed to be based on observations of phenomena. Similarly, children come to school with their own ideas, and learning science is often about students replacing *their* old ideas with new ones. Just like scientists, the changes are most likely to happen when students are presented with observations contradicting their prior beliefs, challenging their mental models, and then being offered alternative ideas. Learning happens when students change their ideas, and science happens when scientists change theirs.

> **Key Takeaway**
> Learning happens when students change their ideas, and science happens when scientists change theirs.

Additional Resources

To learn more about batteries and bulbs, see the lessons retrieved from www.teachengineering.org/view_activity.php?url=collection/cub_/activities/cub_electricity/cub_electricity_lesson05_activity1.xml. A follow-up unit helping students develop models for electrical current, voltage, and resistance within their circuits can be retrieved from www.education.leeds.ac.uk/assets/files/research/cssme/ns-tu/explaining_how_electric_circuits_work.pdf. I retrieved additional information about children's models of circuits at www.education.vic.gov.au/school/teachers/teachingresources/discipline/science/continuum/Pages/electriccircuit.aspx and www.practicalphysics.org/models-electric-circuits.html.

See also Ashmann, S. (2009, December). The pennies-as-electrons analogy. *Science and Children, 47*(4), 24-27.

Chapter 3

I've Got a Theory About That

How do scientists explain observations?

In this section, you will come to see how

- scientists create different kinds of knowledge, and
- theories and laws serve different purposes.

You will be able to help your students

- make and test predictions,
- recognize data are different from their explanation, and
- plan science fair investigations.

In the last chapter, I discussed models—intuitive mental models students bring to the classroom and also models scientists use to explain observations. More than once I referred to the NGSS Appendix H understanding "Science models, laws, mechanisms, and theories explain natural phenomena." We often discuss these words as if they mean more or less the same thing. In everyday life, for example, we talk about a "theory" as an educated guess, perhaps a lightly tested idea that has not yet garnered enough support to be classified as a "law." It's as if there's nothing particularly different about a theory and a law, one just has more support than the other. With enough evidence, any theory could someday be called a law.

This always bothers those of us who study what science is and how science works. We recognize that science and scientists create fundamentally different kinds of knowledge. This means also that scientists—and students doing investigation activities—must also be using varied kinds of methods and skills. Science is not about a step-by-step linear method. No, science is more open-ended than that—more creative and more fun!

OBSERVING DIFFERS FROM EXPLAINING

To show you what I mean about different kinds of knowledge, consider this example. In 2012, *Harvard Magazine* reported on a study where researchers looked at data about violent behavior among high school students (Gudrais, 2012). The study's raw data were a survey completed by about 1,900 students. By itself, the information is just lines in a spreadsheet. But creative researchers recognized a pattern in the data, a correlation.

Key Takeaway

Finding patterns in raw data is a creative activity.

Students drinking a lot of sugary soda each week seemed to be more violent than those who did not. They were more likely to have behaved violently toward peers, another child in their families, and someone they were dating.

Our first thought is always to wonder why—why would kids drinking sugary beverages be violent? I can think of multiple ways to explain the pattern.

- Maybe all that sugar changes kids' behaviors; they get hyperactive, attention spans decrease, and impulsive behavior increases.
- Or maybe it's not that sugar leads to violence, maybe the violent tendencies came first—violent kids love sugar.
- Or maybe an environment that fosters violent behavior just happens to also be one discouraging healthy eating habits. Left unsupervised, children choose sweet sugary beverages and learn to resolve problems through violence.

The same generalization can be explained multiple ways. We cannot yet say one of the explanations is right and the other two are wrong. We have at least three explanations for the same data. The recognition of a link, or correlation, between sugary drinks and violence does not mean the drinks *caused* the violent behavior.

The raw *data* (survey responses), *generalization* that came from the data (sugar is linked with violence), and *explanations* for the generalization are *separate* things. They were created by different people, using different thought processes, and their validities would be tested different ways. Figuring out a procedure to test a question, interpreting the resulting data, and explaining any patterns observed, are different kinds of mental activities. You, your students, and individual scientists may very well be more skilled at one mental activity than another.

Testing whether the correlation is more generally true—remember, science strives for more general and universal ideas—would involve repeating the survey in other places. Testing whether soda *causes* violent behavior would need a different kind of study, perhaps testing the prediction that making non-soda-drinking children consume large quantities of soda pop would make them more violent than they were before drinking the soda, although that's so unethical and unlikely that scientists would ultimately need some other investigation to test the potential causal relationship.

Let's see how these same differences are illustrated during an investigation activity.

Melting Ice

Overview: Students are surprised to observe ice melting faster on metal than on wood or plastic. They go on to investigate how fast ice melts on other substances, looking for patterns.

Grades: Elementary students can focus on investigating the operational questions in Steps 1–5 if the abstract scientific explanation is omitted. Middle school students can benefit from the entire activity.

Time needed: 40–60 minutes. If time is constrained, students can observe Steps 1–3 or 4 one day and complete the activity the next day.

MATERIALS

- Small blocks of metal, wood, plastic, and any other insulators or conductors on which ice cubes can be placed in Step 5 (commercially made materials are available, but just about any pieces of metal, wood, or plastic will work OK)
- Ice cubes, bowls for holding the cubes
- Paper towels
- Scales or balances to ensure ice pieces are similar masses (optional)
- Infrared thermometer to confirm metal and plastic/wood are same temperature (optional)

INSTRUCTIONS

1. Show students blocks of metal and either wood or plastic. If it's at all possible, let the students touch the materials, too.

2. Pull out a bowl of ice cubes and ask students what they think would happen if an ice cube was put on each block. Ask the students whether they think (a) the ice on the metal would melt fastest, (b) the ice on the wood or plastic would melt fastest, or (c) the two cubes would melt at the same rate? Follow up by asking, "Why do you think so?"

3. Having solicited predictions, ideas, and explanations, it's time to find out what actually happens! Whether as a teacher demonstration or students trying on their own, put ice on metal and wood, observe, and have students make notes on observations. (Perhaps first reminding students science is about finding answers via investigations.)

4. Discuss with students what they observed and what they think is going on.

5. Provide students with ice, metal, and wood (or plastic). Beside metal and wood or plastic (for example you can use metal pots and plastic cutting boards), give them other materials onto which they can put an ice cube, such as a variety of metals (conductors) and materials like plastic, glass, and/or ceramics (insulators). Task students with figuring out which materials melt ice quickly and which do not.

6. Group student observations and findings to introduce the concepts of conductors and insulators. Older students can also be introduced to the scientific explanation.

What's Happening? Heat is conducted more efficiently to the ice from conductors, like metals, than insulators, like wood, plastic, and glass.

NGSS Connections: Performance Expectation MS-PS3-4 says students who demonstrate understanding can plan an investigation to determine the relationships among the energy transferred, the type of matter, the mass, and the change in the average kinetic energy of the particles as measured by the temperature of the sample.

TRY IT!

Although technically not a 5E or learning cycle, this lesson incorporates elements of the model. When students observe the unexpected differences in how ice melts on metal and wood or plastic (Step 3), they're *engaged* in the lesson. They continue on to *explore* ideas for themselves (Step 5). The teacher then gathers students' observations and ideas and *introduces new concepts* (conductors and insulators for younger students; energy transfer, as well, for older students) that students have experienced for themselves (Step 6). I don't discuss it here, but to make this activity a full-fledged 5E or learning-cycle lessons, students would go on to use their learning in a new context, which could range from answering application questions to solving problems or even another hands-on activity about heat conduction.

TEACHING TIPS

Step 1: See if students notice that the metal block feels colder than the plastic one. It's unintuitive that the two items will actually both be at room temperature (an observation confirmable, eventually, via an optional infrared thermometer). There is no need to share temperature info with students yet, though.

Step 2: This step (combined with the previous) is ultimately about getting students to think about and commit to a prediction, based on their ideas about what will happen. Some teachers like to solicit verbal responses from individual students, some prefer students write their predictions, and some prefer students discuss their thinking in pairs or small groups before committing to an outcome. Whichever method is used, however, I suggest

- soliciting responses from multiple students, and
- following up by asking "Why do you think so?"

These are ways to increase participation and better understand student thinking. Understanding students' preconceived ideas is the starting point for conceptual change.

Steps 3: As with any demonstration or investigation activity, you should have already tried this for yourself. Most of us would predict we would see two ice cubes slowly melting. Because the metal feels colder to the touch than plastic, wood, or ceramic, we might predict ice would melt a bit slower on the cool feeling metal.

Quickly, however, it's clear the ice is melting faster on the metal than the plastic or wood. Science educators call demonstrations where results fly in the face of

> **Key Takeaway**
>
> Try investigation activities on your own before teaching them to students for the first time.

expectations based on common sense *discrepant events*. Common sense often predicts something different than what's observed. Seeing such a marked difference in the rate ice melts is, for most of us, a discrepant event. (Watching milk swirl in the Milk Fireworks activity is also a discrepant event.)

A discrepant event is a demonstration that produces an unexpected outcome, something differing from what students' previous experiences would lead them to believe was true.

Step 5: Students now go on to do their own investigation activities, examining how ice melts when put on top of various materials, after trying the demo out on metal and plastic or wood, replicating what the teacher did. Trying out the procedure the way the teacher did, and getting similar results, serves as a kind of check for understanding that students understand the procedure you'd like them to follow. Students might even test the possibility of a sneaky teacher trick by moving the unmelted cube on the wood over to the metal—only to find the cube now starts melting faster than it was on wood. After observing cubes on metal and wood or plastic, however, they take over and try the procedure out on new materials.

This would be a good activity for pairs or, possibly, groups of three students. Larger groups might go off task as too many students don't really have anything to do.

One of the things you can do during the activity is provide guidance by discussing with students what they would need to do to assure their test was "fair," like making sure to choose two ice cubes that seem identical. Indeed, students might have other ideas they would like to test.

Throughout the investigations, the teacher's role (beyond managing the classroom) involves

- asking students about what they're doing ("Tell me about what you're doing"),
- accepting their responses ("OK"), and
- following up by asking students to explain their procedures ("Why did you decide to do that?" or "What were you trying to find out?"), which spurs further conversation.
- The teacher also can provide subtle hints to help increase the chances investigations are fruitful. Often this involves asking students to make predictions. ("Suppose you were to do ___. What do you think would happen? . . . How can you find out?").
- Interacting with students also allows the teacher to tell students explicitly how their actions parallel those of other scientists (pointing out when students are engaged in science practices), teaching students lessons about what science is and how science works.

Key Takeaway

These teacher behaviors are useful and suggested for just about all investigation activities.

Students will presumably come to accept—as a conclusion to their experiments—the general pattern or description that ice melts faster sitting on metallic materials than plastic, wood, ceramic, or glass materials.

WHAT'S GOING ON IN THE SCIENCE?

Disciplinary Core Ideas PS3A and PS3B are about energy and its movement from place to place. MS-PS3-4's clarification statement mentions experiments with ice melting and the cooling or heating of various materials:

> Examples of experiments could include comparing final water temperatures after different masses of ice melted in the same volume of water with the same initial temperature, the temperature change of samples of different materials with the same mass as they cool or heat in the environment, or the same material with different masses when a specific amount of energy is added.

At the end of the activity, we are all still left wondering *why* ice melted faster on metal than on wood or plastic. The generalization about materials on which ice melts faster or slower is a different type of knowledge than the accepted explanation underlying the observations. It's an explanation that cannot be directly developed via hands-on classroom activities. As with many scientific explanations or models, things quickly get abstract.

Many other observations and generalizations have led scientists to accept an overarching explanation—a scientific theory, actually. It starts with a model in which everything is made of invisibly tiny particles constantly moving around (molecules, atoms, etc.). It's part of the same model we used to explain what was happening with voltage and current in electrical circuits.

The explanation includes the idea that energy is being transferred from the metal or plastic to the ice. The way it's modeled, when objects hold a lot of (heat) energy—when they are warmer—the particles making up the objects are moving or vibrating more than those making up objects holding less (heat) energy (National Research Council, 2012, p. 120).

When molecules collide, they transfer energy; when a fast particle hits a slow particle, the fast particle ends up moving a little more slowly and the slow particle ends up moving a little faster. In the case of our ice, the chunks of metal and plastic are warmer—their molecules, on average, are moving around faster—than those of the ice. When the faster moving particles meet the slower moving particles, the resulting collisions leave ice particles moving a little faster (the ice warms) and the metal and wood particles moving a little slower (the metal and wood cool). Scientists call the process (heat) *conduction*.

The same explanation predicts and explains why conduction depends on temperature differences, how large the items are and how much of them are in contact with one another, what else is in the surroundings, and—last but not least—properties of the materials themselves. Some objects are really good at transferring heat energy—they are good heat conductors—others are not. Metals, as it turns out, are good heat conductors; plastic and wood are not.

As one might predict (and test) from this model, if few particles are bouncing around, a substance would be a poor heat conductor. Vacuums don't conduct heat at all, and gases (with many fewer particles per unit area than liquids or solids) are usually poor conductors. Double-pained windows with little or no air in between the panes are very poor conductors—that means they do a great job at making sure heat energy does not leave your home. Similarly, fur, feathers, and "puffy" fibers trap air, and air is a poor conductor, so these materials do a good job keeping warmth from escaping on a cold day!

CONNECTIONS TO THE NATURE OF SCIENCE

Watching the ice melt, we all ask the same questions, whether scientists or children: "Why?" "What's going on?" We observe something unexpected, cool, or otherwise personally intriguing (a pattern, generalization, or similar description), and we wonder why (i.e., search for an explanation). We wonder why the ice melted faster on the metal, why soda pop consumption is linked to violent behavior, and why the milk swirled (Chapter 1). In each case, we try to explain what we observed. And just like recognizing a pattern amongst soda pop drinkers is different than explaining the why behind the pattern, recognizing ice melts faster on metal than wood, or milk swirls faster when it's warm, is different than explaining the why behind the pattern.

It may seem seamless, but three separate mental processes are actually going on here. Watching the ice melt is collecting data, noticing differences in how it melts on different surfaces is analyzing and interpreting data, and trying to explain the mechanism behind what's going on is another kind of interpretation.

> **NGSS Connection:** SEP4 Analyzing and interpreting data

When scientists wonder why, and think about explanations, they must ultimately go a step further and test their explanations. Thinking about what's happening leads to other investigations. In school, science investigation activities end cleanly. Exigencies of schooling regularly prohibit anything else, but this is one way school science often differs from the activities of scientists.

For scientists, data from one investigation often lead to another question for another investigation. If students move from observing a demonstration to planning and carrying out their own investigations, they are more accurately acting like professional scientists than typically seen in school science experiences. In the case of our ice melting investigation activity, when students consider what they think will happen when they put ice on different materials—when they make predictions, in other words—and then create tests to find out whether observations support their ideas, they are mimicking scientists, while learning themselves. If results testing one question lead them to try something else, that's even better!

PRACTICES IN PRACTICE

Although student investigations *always* involve multiple SEPs, the performance expectation I mentioned in connection with this activity (MS-PS3-4) begins with "Students who demonstrate understanding can plan an investigation to determine the relationships among. . . . " This is a reference to SEP3 *planning and carrying out investigations.* Students working on investigations where they are trying to learn more about how or why ice melts at different rates on different materials are asking investigable questions, planning and carrying out investigations, and—when they see what happens—analyzing and interpreting their data.

In general, students will be more successful planning and carrying out investigations if the data they collect involve something both tangible and familiar. Everything students use in this investigation activity (as well as others in this book) should be familiar to most students. That said, NGSS's Appendix F provides additional clues about differing expectations for students in Grades 3–5 vs. 6–8 regarding this practice:

- **In the 3–5 classroom:** Generally speaking, younger students will need more teacher structuring than older students. They can understand, plan, and carry out investigations involving fair testing, which means at some level they can understand the concepts of controlled variables and the need to consider how many times a test has been repeated. They can also make predictions about what they believe would happen if a variable was changed, and then carry out investigations to test their thinking. (In this activity, comparing equal sized pieces of ice would be an example of a controlled variable that makes tests more "fair.")

- **In the 6–8 classroom:** All else being equal, older and more capable students can plan and carry out investigations at a slightly more sophisticated level and with less teacher structuring than their younger counterparts. Instead of talking only about fair testing, Grade 6–8 teachers can discuss independent and dependent variables, as well as controlled variables. The *independent variable* is the thing you are testing or changing, and the *dependent variable* is the thing you are measuring or observing as a result of changing the independent variable. In this investigation, the wood, metal, plastic, etc. is the independent variable, and ice-melting speed is the dependent variable. *Controlled variables* are the things you consciously keep the same to make your tests fairer. Older students are also more capable of evaluating different ways of collecting data.

ADDENDA: THEORIES, LAWS, AND HYPOTHESES

As a Grade 3–8 teacher, it probably meets expectations if your students leave school recognizing the difference between observing, seeing potential patterns or generalizations, explaining what was observed, and recognizing that continued curiosity spurs further investigation. This differs from a caricature of science where scientists always follow a rigid multistep method, get a result, create conclusions . . . and call it a day. That's an unfair exaggeration, but it's one my colleagues and I often hear.

As a teacher, however, you need deeper understanding than your students. You'll feel more comfortable, more confident, more able to pay attention to your students' needs if unconcerned with your own understanding of what you are teaching.

I started the chapter by mentioning the NGSS nature of science understanding that "Scientific models, laws, mechanisms, and theories explain natural phenomena." Now I can return to it and connect it with my discussion of the melting-ice activity. When we say ice melts faster on conductors than insulators, we're actually expressing a scientific law (or at least a law-like statement). And our explanation, the one with invisibly tiny particles (atoms or molecules) bumping into each other, is based on a scientific theory.

Independent variable is the factor the experimenter is consciously changing or testing; it's the thing he or she is trying to find out about.

Dependent variable is the measurement or observation being recorded as a result of changing the independent variable; it's the experiment's outcome data.

Controlled variables are factors in an experiment the experimenter consciously keeps the same to assure a fair test; ideally, the independent variable is the only difference between groups being tested.

Key Takeaway

Scientific models, laws, mechanisms, and theories explain natural phenomena. —NGSS Appendix H

Scientific theory is a broad explanation for some aspect of the natural world; strong theories are well substantiated by their abilities to explain and accurately predict a wide range of phenomena.

Scientific law is a generalization or description of repeated observations.

> **Key takeaway**
>
> A scientific theory is a broad explanation, while a scientific law is a generalization or description. Descriptions and explanations are different things.

A *scientific theory* is a broad explanation encompassing lots of data, while a *scientific law* is a generalization or description of data. Among other things, scientific theories explain laws. They are different things.

This may be a bit confusing if you were taught that hypotheses are tentative untested ideas, theories are hypotheses that have been tested a little, and laws are hypotheses that have been tested a lot—hypotheses become theories, and theories become laws. But, really, that's just plain wrong. The words may be used that way *outside* science, but they have different meanings *inside* science.

Let me show you what I mean. Here's a list of some well-known scientific theories:

- The theory of evolution via natural selection
- The Big Bang theory
- The theory of relativity
- Quantum theory
- Plate tectonic theory
- Climate change theories
- The germ theory of disease transmission
- Cell theory
- Atomic and kinetic-molecular theories (underlying the explanations about our melting ice and electrical current)
- Gravitational theory

What stands out in lists like this is how important the ideas are to their disciplines. Geology is almost entirely based on plate tectonic theory, chemistry on the atomic and kinetic-molecular theories, the infectious disease branch of medicine on the germ theory, etc. These are not educated guesses or lightly tested hypotheses.

Scientific theories stand at the roots of their disciplines. They are the big ideas, the broad *explanations* that withstood all sorts of testing. I used the kinetic-molecular theory when explaining both conduction and melting ice, and also electrical current. Scientific theories guide and influence how scientists understand, explain, and think about their disciplines. The best theories even allow scientists to make testable predictions about things no one has yet observed.

The *Science Framework* that guided the development of NGSS accents not only the importance of scientific theories, but also the recognition theories are broad explanations:

> The goal of science is the construction of theories that provide explanatory accounts of the world. A theory becomes accepted when

it has multiple lines of empirical evidence and greater explanatory power of phenomena than previous theories. (National Research Council, 2012, p. 52)

What is it these theories are explaining? They are explaining all sorts of generalizations, and the generalizations are what we mean when using the term *scientific law*.

A scientific theory can never become a scientific law, because they are different things. Generalizations ("Metals are good heat conductors, plastics are not"; "children drinking sugary beverages show violent tendencies") and explanations

> **Key Takeaway**
>
> Scientific theories never, ever turn into scientific laws.

of the generalizations are different kinds of knowledge. So, the Theory of Evolution by Natural Selection will never be renamed the "Law of Evolution by Natural Selection" and geology's Law of Superposition was never called the "Theory of Superposition."

Like theory and law, the word *hypothesis* is sometimes used differently inside and outside science. Like most of my peers, I define the term hypothesis to refer to scientific claims that have not yet been put to the test. Untested theories and untested laws start as hypotheses.

Hypotheses are investigable scientific claims; they can be theory-like explanations or law-like generalizations.

Returning to Chapter 1, when students observe the Milk Fireworks demonstration they may notice what they believe are patterns in how and when the milk swirls. They are forming hypotheses. If they and their peers test and retest a hypothesis we might say it's now a scientific law (or, more accurately, a law-like statement; true laws usually cover a wider variety of observations). Gifted students who learn about surface tension, the properties of water, and explanation for the swirling behavior that involves characteristics of water molecules would be learning about the scientific theory explaining a scientific law.

ONE LAST EXAMPLE: SCIENCE FAIRS

Schools sometimes use the word *hypothesis* as if it's synonymous with *predictions*. I think this probably comes out most strongly during science fair season. For those of you helping students with science fair projects, I end the chapter by considering examples of science fair questions students could investigate, assuming the students were then instructed to record their hypotheses, procedures, and results. Remember, the *hypothesis* is the general or overarching scientific claim

> **Key Takeaway**
>
> Hypotheses, when tested, lead directly to predictions—but they are subtly different things.

being investigated. The *prediction* is what the student thinks will happen when a specific investigation procedure is followed. I googled "science fair questions," and the first hit I got included these three questions:

1. Where are the most germs in your school?
2. Which brand of paper towel is the strongest?
3. Do athletic students have better lung capacity than nonathletic students?

There are lots of hypotheses and predictions you might have considered for each of these questions. Here are examples I came up with.

1. "Where are the most germs in your school?"

A student could say "I think the most germs will be in the bathrooms." This is a *prediction*.

When a student provides a prediction, asking "Why do you think so?" will often help the teacher elucidate an underlying hypothesis in the student's mind. In this case, an underlying hypothesis being tested might be that microorganisms grow most efficiently or quickly in warm, moist places. If this (law-like) hypothesis is supported, we would predict that when samples are cultured from around the school, the most germs would be found in bathrooms, kitchens, and any other comparatively warm and moist spots.

Parenthetically, to get away from the common "I was right" or "I was wrong" attitudes students often have after performing their investigations, an alternative is for students to initially consider *two* or more possible investigation outcomes and what they would mean. In the current example, one outcome from the student's investigation might be more microorganisms in the kitchen and bathroom than anywhere else, supporting the idea germs grow well under these conditions. Another outcome could be the data showing the kitchen and bathroom *not* having more microorganisms than anywhere else, seemingly supporting the idea microorganisms grow best under other conditions. Both outcomes are scientifically valid and important; both outcomes can lead to further investigations. Results other than those hoped for may sometimes be disappointing, but they are not "wrong."

> **Key Takeaway**
>
> Results are not scientifically bad or wrong just because they are disappointing.

2. "Which brand of paper towel is the strongest?"

Instructed to "write your hypothesis," a student jots "I think <Brand1> is the strongest." As before, this is actually a *prediction* and, as before, it's tied in with the details of the investigation procedure the student is going to use. Asked why she picked Brand1, the student might say "because it's the thickest." The student may believe thicker paper towels are stronger than thinner towels. This is the (law-like) *hypothesis* the student is testing. As in the last example, the student could begin her investigation with two or more possible outcomes in mind, considering what each would mean about paper towel strength.

3. "Do athletic students have better lung capacity than nonathletic students?"

The student wants to investigate the *hypothesis* regular athletic activity increases lung capacity. The student's procedure might be to have athletes and nonathletes blow as much as they can into bags, measuring the volume of expelled air, and the student might *predict* athletes' lung capacities would be higher than those of nonathletes.

Keep in mind, when data support a hypothesis it does not mean the hypothesis has been proven right. As in the case of the violent soda pop drinkers, *other* hypotheses could also be supported. Maybe musicians playing horns, trumpets, and other wind instruments have large lung capacities—even if they are nonathletic. The same data might be explained multiple ways, since data and its explanation are different things. The marching band playing at half-time may have stronger lungs than the football players! Of course, the only way to know for sure would be . . . another investigation.

CONCLUSION

In the previous two chapters, I've discussed how science is based on observations, empirical evidence. Our intuitive commonsense understandings of the world are also based on evidence. Science, however, differs because it's also interested in general, universal truths (laws) and broadly applicable, overarching explanations (theories).

NGSS's Appendix H says "scientific investigations use a variety of methods." This chapter helps explain why that is so. Scientific investigations use a variety of methods because science is ultimately about generating and investigating a variety of knowledge types. Each requires subtly different skills, talents, and abilities. Science is a more diverse activity than sometimes portrayed. This helps make it fun and interesting.

The next chapter continues with more discussion and detail about science's different methods, distinguishing differences in how generalizations (laws) and explanations (theories) are tested.

Key Takeaway

Scientific investigations use a variety of methods. —NGSS Appendix H

Additional Resources

To learn more about this chapter's demonstration and its scientific explanation, see the chapter "Party Meltdown," pp. 105–112, in Richard Konicek-Moran's *Everyday physical science mysteries: Stories for inquiry-based science teaching*, Arlington, VA: NSTA Press, 2013. Konicek, with Bruce Watson (1990), also wrote a wonderful article about heat, temperature, and conceptual change. The Nuffield Foundation has a nice lesson plan online at www.nuffieldfoundation.org/sites/default/files/files/Melting%20ice%20-%20merged%20PDF.pdf; note how the activity described here is slightly different from the Nuffield version.

Chapter 4

Elementary, My Dear Watson

Why is there no such thing as the scientific method?

In this section, you will come to see how

- scientists use a variety of methods, including inductive and deductive reasoning, to answer questions; and
- no single method leads to sure knowledge; one investigation cannot prove an idea.

You will be able to

- help your students learn inductively, searching for patterns in observations;
- help your students learn deductively, making and testing predictions; and
- use discrepant events to engage student attention.

OK, forgive the flippancy of the chapter subtitle. At some really broad level, a scientific method exists—ask a question or come up with an idea that's testable empirically, test it, see what you find, modify your thinking if necessary, repeat, convince the scientific community. But that's an encompassing description that addresses lots of things. Those of us who study what science is and how science works don't like the implication that scientific investigations all follow a 4-to-8 linear-step method the way students are often taught in school. Although scientific investigations are limited to addressing questions answerable with empirical data, scientists work with different types of data—observations, generalizations, explanations, etc.—which implies differences in methods for creating or testing them. Scientific disciplines may also have their own ways of doing things. Sometimes, differences exist even within disciplines. For example, biochemists and wetland ecologists are both biologists, but they tend to approach problems a little differently. The same can be said when comparing theoretical and experimental physicists.

So what are these various "methods"? In this chapter, I focus on two ways of thinking scientists use when figuring out how nature works—inductive and deductive reasoning, along with two investigation activities illustrating the methods. Children and scientists *both* use these methods to understand the world around them. Recognizing, understanding, and appreciating their strengths and limitations goes a long way toward helping you understand what science is and how science works.

INDUCTIVE REASONING

One way scientists learn new things is via a process called ***inductive reasoning***. When thinking inductively, we use details, observations, or other individual bits of information to generalize more broadly. We watch the sun rise day after day (individual observations), and come to trust the sun will continue to rise every day (the broader generalization). We see a flash of lightning and then hear a crash of thunder. When we see and hear the same flashes and crashes again and again, we conclude thunder follows lightning. We push a funny looking button on a remote control and our TV unexpectedly turns off. When the same thing happens again the next day, and the day after that, we conclude the button turns off the TV. The three times we pressed the button were individual observations. Our inference the button turns off the TV is the broader generalization.

Inductive reasoning is the activity of using details, observations, and other information to make a generalization.

Inductive reasoning is important, yet rarely emphasized in school. The authors of the *Science Framework* recognize that's wrong:

> Although there is no universal agreement about teaching the nature of science, there is a strong consensus about characteristics of the

scientific enterprise that should be understood by an educated citizen. For example, the notion that there is a single scientific method of observation, hypothesis, deduction, and conclusion—a myth perpetuated to this day by many textbooks—is fundamentally wrong. Scientists do use deductive reasoning, but they *also search for patterns, classify different objects, make generalizations from repeated observations, and engage in a process of making inferences as to what might be the best explanation.* Thus the picture of scientific reasoning is richer, more complex, and more diverse than the image of a linear and unitary scientific method would suggest. (National Research Council, 2012, p. 78; emphasis added)

Scientists find or create law-like generalizations by reasoning inductively, and so can students. In the classic sinking and floating activity, students describe and classify materials by whether they sink or float when placed in water. Young children have been performing the activity since at least the 1960s, when the Elementary Science Study (1968) first published its *Sink and Float* curriculum. The basic curriculum is still appropriate and popular today.

ACTIVITY 4

Sinking and Floating

Overview: Students observe objects that sink or float, inductively learning properties that help them predict and understand flotation.

Grades: This activity is appropriate for all grade levels 3–8. Middle school students, however, can probably complete the activity more quickly than younger ones, and continue the investigation (as discussed below) by investigating density and learning to predict mathematically whether an object is likely to sink or float in ways younger students cannot.

Time needed: 20–60 minutes for the basic activity described below; extensions add additional time.

MATERIALS

Each student group typically needs

- Ten to twelve everyday materials, including some that sink and other that float. Examples include objects made of wood (toothpick, pencil, etc.), metal (aluminum foil, BBs, and other small objects made of various kinds of metals), plastic (plastic bottles, toy blocks, plastic forks, etc.) and objects like sponges, rubber balls, Styrofoam blocks, rocks, various types of fruit, soda cans, and paper
- Two to four different sizes of the same object for testing, for example, two to four different sized pieces of sponge or Styrofoam, two to four metal balls that are different sizes, etc.
- A large water-filled bowl
- Notebooks for data recording
- Scales or balances (if you wish to extend the activity by having students analyze and interpret quantitative measurements about "heavy" and "light" objects. Using mathematics and computational thinking is one of NGSS's science and engineering practices.)

INSTRUCTIONS

1. The activity begins with something to engage students' thinking and predicting whether particular objects sink or float when put in a tub or pan of water. For young children, it could be a story, like Pamela Allen's *Who Sank the Boat?* (Allen, 1996).

   Alternatively, I like the engagement that comes from a discrepant event. Watching a light object (like a small metal ball) sink and a heavier object (like a large wooden ball) float can prove appropriately perplexing to students expecting larger or heavier objects to sink. Perform the demonstration, watching and listening for student reactions.

2. Show students other objects and ask them to make predictions about whether they think the objects will sink or float.

3. After each student in the group predicts whether they think an object will sink or float (and, if you like, writes the predictions in their notebooks), they find out by placing the objects in water. Students work at their own pace, perhaps testing the materials in their own orders, and also possibly changing their initial predictions about whether a particular object would sink or float as the activity continues.

4. Discuss with students differences they noted between objects that did and did not float, using group data to help students categorize the objects according to their properties, for example, wood generally floats and metal generally sinks, regardless of the material's size or shape.

5. The teacher can then bring out new materials with similar characteristics, for example, other kinds of wood or metal, other common and familiar materials, etc. and ask students again to predict whether they think the object fits better in the category with objects that floated or those that sank. Predictions, of course, are then tested.

What's Happening? Objects denser than the water they're put in sink; those less dense than the water they're put in float. Density is the ratio of mass to volume, or how heavy something is "for its size."

NGSS Connections: Performance expectation 2-PS1-1 says students who demonstrate understanding can plan and conduct an investigation to describe and classify different kinds of materials by their observable properties. (The observable property, in this case, is floating.)

In addition, performance expectation MS-PS1-2 (which is actually about analyzing and interpreting data about the properties of substances before and after chemical reactions) notes specifically in its assessment boundary that "assessment is limited to analysis of the following properties: density, melting point. . . . " Clearly, investigations related to density must fall under NGSS expectations.

TRY IT!

This activity fits well with some elements of the 5E or learning-cycle model. A discrepant event in Step 1 *engages* student interest. As students go on to predict and then find out whether various objects float (Steps 2 and 3), students are *exploring*, and the teacher has the chance to learn about their preconceived ideas. By the end of Step 4, students will have categorized observations into objects that do and do not float, which serves as a kind of *explanation* phase (especially if words like "floater," "sinker," and/or "property" are introduced). Students then use their new learning, the **expansion** phase of the cycle, when predicting what other objects will do when placed in water.

Steps 2–3 and 5 would appear similar to an observer. Essentially, it looks like students explore, are introduced to new ideas, and then explore some more. What's different, in this instance, between the exploratory and expansion activity is the students. It's not visible, but in the first part of the activity they are brainstorming and exploring their preconceived ideas, and in the latter part, they are testing their new learning.

TEACHING TIPS

Step 1: Here are some suggestions to make discrepant events, performed as demonstrations, as engaging as possible:

- Ask students to make predictions before performing the demonstration by saying, "What do you think will happen when I drop these two objects in the water?"
- Acknowledge responses, to encourage continued participation ("Thank you for your answer.") and—if you feel it's appropriate—follow up by asking students for an explanation ("Why do you think so?").
- Further encourage participation and discussion by soliciting predictions and explanations from additional students. You could ask, "Who has a different idea they'd like to share?"

The more objects available, the more likely students are to inductively create their own generalizations. Students often believe (a) light things float, heavy things sink and (b) floating is caused by the presence of air. (You'll confirm whether your students hold similar ideas when asking things like "tell me about what you think is happening here.") Recognizing these common misconceptions is useful when choosing objects for students to test. Choosing some things whose behavior will challenge a misconception can spark both interest and learning (see Yin, Tomita, & Shavelson, 2008). So keep an eye out for light objects that sink, heavy objects that float, objects with air that sink, and objects without air that float. Among the surprising examples teachers commonly use are sugared and unsugared sodas, peeled and unpeeled oranges, and Snickers and Three Musketeers brands of chocolate bars. In each case, one of the items floats and the other sinks. (Hint: remove as much pith as possible from the orange.)

Step 2: Solicit student ideas about differences they notice between objects that float and sink in water. In offering explanations, students may begin revealing mental models guiding their predictions.

After brainstorming lists as a class, it's time for hands-on investigation!

Step 3: Sometimes the investigation activity is done mostly by the teacher as a demonstration—he or she shows students an object, asks them to predict whether they think it will sink or float, and then puts the object in water for everyone to see what happened. Or a student volunteer can put objects in water, while the teacher continues to lead the discussion. I think the investigation activity is more powerful when students place the objects in water by themselves, at their own pace and order, noticing up close what happens. I recognize, however, sometimes this may not be feasible.

While this investigation activity most closely aligns, perhaps, with a second grade performance expectation, it is both appropriate and challenging (with minor modifications) for older students, too. (Many smart, able college students still find this activity engaging and challenging.)

Your students might also find the mass of each object before putting it in the water. You can return to this numerical data later, challenging the idea that heavy things sink and light things float.

As your students make, test, and discuss predictions, the teacher's role is critical—listening, questioning, and subtly suggesting ideas (while simultaneously managing the classroom). The skillful teacher asks questions or says things that ultimately help students understand sinking and floating, as well as the nature of science and science practices, without simply telling "the answers." A teacher might be heard saying

- "Tell me about the differences you are seeing between things that sink and things that float," followed by statements paraphrasing or clarifying students' statements, or
- "What do you think would happen if we dropped <some object> in the water?" followed by "Why do you think so?"

For middle school students, Sinking and Floating is often linked to learning about density. (Some schools and curricula introduce the concept of density at younger ages.) I believe truly understanding the concept, beyond memorizing an algorithm to divide mass by volume, requires more abstract reasoning than many younger children possess. Use your own judgment and knowledge about your students to determine what is most appropriate for their abilities.

As an example of inductive reasoning with children in younger grades, I focused on this first part of traditional sinking and floating activities. It typically continues beyond what I mentioned (see, for example, McDonald, 2012, or Smithenry & Kim, 2010; Keeley [2013] describes an activity where students predict and observe what will happen to objects before and after holes are punched in them.).

Students often investigate materials whose sinking or floating behavior varies—or doesn't—depending on how they are shaped. A common investigation activity involves taking a lump of clay (which sinks) and trying to shape it so it floats. The investigation—or engineering design—activity is often even called "clay boats."

Sinking and Floating
(continued)

Time needed: 30–60 minutes

MATERIALS

Each student group typically needs

- Florist's clay, or similar shapeable clay-like material that will not dissolve in water; enough for each student to have a lump about half the size of a fist
- Pennies, small washers, or similar materials that could be put inside the clay "boats"
- A large water-filled bowl
- Notebooks for data recording

INSTRUCTIONS

1. Show students that a lump of clay sinks, if they have not already observed this.

2. Have students reshape their clay to make the same piece of clay float. I suggest they note shapes that sank as well as those that floated.

3. Once students have molded clay into a shape that floats, challenge them to mold the clay so it will not only float, but also hold weight inside, that is, carry a load. Again, students can record how well their designs worked for carrying a load.

FIGURE 4.1 Sinking and Floating

The same clay can be molded to float or sink.

WHAT'S GOING ON IN THE SCIENCE?

Typically, children believe "light" things float and "heavy" things sink. We all recognize lots of light objects that sink, while massive ocean liners float. A developmentally appropriate way to better approach what's going on is to tell children objects that are "heavy for their size" often sink, while those "light for their size" tend to float. This at least starts down the road to helping students understand floating and sinking are linked to *both* an object's weight (mass, more accurately) *and* its size (volume). The more mass is packed into a given volume the more likely an object is to sink.

Children also believe air makes things float, that is, things that float must have air inside. This commonsense explanation fits many everyday observations and is a little difficult to challenge when people talk about air being inside objects (and therefore invisible). Scientists would nevertheless challenge the assertion with counterexamples (oil, for example, floats on water—even though there's no air in oil).

Ultimately, density is the scientific measure for how tightly packed together the material is making up an object. Objects that are denser, scientists would say, have more matter packed into a given space than objects that are less dense. We measure how much matter is present in an object as its mass, and the space it takes up as its volume. Scientists define density as the ratio of mass to volume. If an object is denser than the water it's placed in, it will sink; if it's less dense, it will float. (Salt water is denser than fresh water; hence, some objects float in salt water that sink in fresh water.) Finally, you can make something like a lump of clay float by shaping it in such a way that it displaces more water. (Asking students to take a lump of florist's clay, which sinks, and reshape the same piece of clay to float is a common part of this investigation activity for older students. Make sure to use florist's clay, not the more typical clay that dissolves in water.) Reshaping a piece of clay does not change its mass, but its volume increases when it takes up more space. If the volume increases, the mass to volume ratio decreases and the object becomes less dense. (The one unfortunate thing about this is the reshaped clay becomes larger by increasing its air space—potentially reinforcing a commonsense misconception.)

PRACTICES IN PRACTICE

On the surface, this seems like a simplistic investigation. And it is. After all, the investigatory procedure is just dropping stuff in a tub of water and seeing whether or not it floats! Young children are certainly capable of doing that. Nevertheless, it still illustrates scientific practices.

NGSS Connection:
SEP3 Planning
and carrying out
investigations

- Children are *planning and carrying out an investigation* when asking and then predicting whether something will float, and then finding out by placing objects in water.

- When observing what happened they *are analyzing data*.
- They *construct explanations* and, when discussing their thoughts with peers or the teacher, engage in what NGSS authors call *argument from evidence*. (The teacher can continually reinforce this last point by asking things like "How do you know this?" and "What evidence do you have?" Similarly, students can be asked to write the evidence for and reasoning behind their ideas.)

NGSS Connection:
SEP4 Analyzing and interpreting data

NGSS Connection:
SEP7 Engaging in argument from evidence

If the teacher explicitly shows students the parallels between their actions and those of scientists, then over time, students will come to better understand science and its practices. (If you think about it, this is another example of learning via inductive reasoning!)

> **Key Takeaway**
>
> Students will better understand science's practices if the teacher explicitly and repeatedly shows students the parallels between their actions and those of scientists.

CONNECTIONS TO THE NATURE OF SCIENCE

When students observe multiple objects sinking or floating, begin recognizing for themselves patterns in properties of objects that float (most plastics and woods) or sink (most metals), and test their thinking by dropping additional objects in water, they are learning and reasoning inductively—like scientists.

Even small children reason inductively. It's a key way they learn. When they exhibit a particular behavior multiple times and come to recognize it is followed by a "time out," they inductively make the generalization that a behavior is linked to punishment. (Or, if they observe the behavior only sometimes to be followed by a parental reaction, they inductively infer it's OK to keep doing it.)

Scientific hypotheses ultimately accepted as "facts" or law-like generalizations are often confirmed via an inductive process. A scientist sees chunks of copper and aluminum acting as heat conductors and inductively infers an idea: Perhaps all metals are good heat conductors. So she tests the heat conductivity of metal after metal after metal. If they all conduct well, she decides metals are good conductors.

NGSS Connection:
Scientists use a variety of methods.

THE PROBLEM WITH INDUCTIVE REASONING

These examples involve simple inductive reasoning. The sun rose on the first, second, third, and fourth day of the month, and we conclude the sun will *always* rise. Copper, aluminum, silver, and gold conduct heat well, and we conclude *all* metals conduct heat well. Children put various pieces of plastic in water and conclude all plastics float.

Have we thus *proven* the sun will always rise, all metals conduct heat well, and all plastics float?

Of course not. We could test the conductivity of more metals and see if the pattern continues to hold. How many would need to be tested before we had proven all metals are good conductors? Ten? A hundred? A thousand? The truth is, barring a test of every bit of metal in the known universe, we can never be sure. The possibility always exists data will show some kind of metal is a poor conductor, disproving the idea.

Inductive reasoning is powerful and ever present. Many key ideas were arrived at inductively and science (and other fields) depends upon it. But it cannot prove anything.

DEDUCTIVE REASONING

Scientific thinking is not limited to inductive reasoning, taking individual observations and inferring general conclusions. We often go the other way, too, starting with general conclusions. In its purest form philosophers call this **deductive reasoning**. Made famous in Sherlock Holmes stories, deductive thinking combines ideas in ways so that if the starting ideas (or premises) are accurate and true, a conclusion is reached that must also be true. It's easier to illustrate than explain.

Deductive reasoning is the activity of using well established general premises to create more specific conclusions; often used when testing explanations by making predictions about specific situations.

Going back to the last section, if *all* metals really are conductors, and copper is a metal, then copper *must* be a conductor. Sometimes deductive reasoning is represented this way:

IF all metals are conductors,

AND copper is a metal

THEN copper is a conductor.

More poetically:

IF the sun always rises every day,

AND tomorrow is another day,

THEN tomorrow the sun will rise.

As an example of deductive reasoning in the classroom, consider the classic *Mystery Powders* activity in which students investigate the properties of various white household powders, ultimately using their learning (deductively) to identify powders whose initial identities are unknown. *Mystery Powders,* like *Sink and Float,* began as units in the Elementary Science Study; both are common, tried and true elementary science units.

Mystery Powders

Overview: Students investigate the properties of common household powders, and then use their knowledge to find the contents of an unknown powder.

Grades: Fifth grade and higher

Time needed: Depends on how many powders you use and the tests you elect to have students perform on their powders. This activity probably takes longer than most, perhaps 2–5 hours total, spread out over multiple days.

MATERIALS

- Surfaces or containers for groups to perform their tests. I have small trays, like you might serve snacks on during a party. Other teachers use small cups, plates, or lids from containers like juice bottles (which helps remind students they need to use only small amounts of each powder).
- Multipound bags or boxes of salt, sugar, baking soda, cornstarch or flour, and talc
- Iodine solution (drugstore iodine solutions diluted with distilled water by a factor of 5–10 parts water to 1 part iodine)
- Vinegar
- Distilled water
- Something like popsicle sticks, toothpicks, or coffee stirrers for mixing powders
- Black construction paper
- Magnifying glasses
- Materials for heating sugar, for example, hot plate(s) or tea light candle(s); aluminum foil—folded into a small cup shape to hold the sugar; clothes pins or tongs, to hold the aluminum foil over the heat source (optional)
- Citric or tartaric acid, and a test solution made by dissolving baking soda in water. Older children can add this additional powder to their tests; citric and tartaric acids will fizz when combined with baking soda solution (optional).
- Some way to provide students with relatively small amounts of each powder and testing liquid. I use old film canisters to hold powders and eye dropper bottles to hold liquids. Other teachers store powders in large zipped bags, dispensing them in paper cups, and store liquids in small jars with lids, giving students eye droppers so they use only small quantities during their testing.

- Newspapers, paper towels, spoons (optional)
- Safety goggles
- Paper towels, all-purpose cleaner, etc. for clean-up
- Student notebooks or Post-It style notes for data recording

INSTRUCTIONS

1. Inform students that their ultimate goal will be to figure out the identity of an unknown white powder.

2. Provide students with small amounts of each powder, dark construction paper, and magnifying glasses. Students can work in pairs, or even individually, while still sharing materials, that is, one set of powders might be shared by multiple students, each of whom is working individually or in pairs, if your classroom setup makes this possible.

   Ask students to see if they can find out anything unique about each of the powders by looking at them (with and without magnifying glasses), touching them, and (if one of your powders is talc) carefully smelling the powders. (Tell students not to taste the powders. Young students might also be instructed about how to smell carefully and safely.)

   Students should be instructed to write their observations. Some teachers tell students precisely what to observe and how to record their observations. Others leave some of this to students' own discretion, perhaps discussing their data as a whole class soon after this step in the activity.

3. The activity continues with students performing similar tests placing a few drops of vinegar on each of the powders and observing what (if anything) happens. (Baking soda usually fizzes.)

4. Students repeat Step 3, investigating how distilled water can help them figure out the identity of their unknown powder. (Some powders readily absorb water; the water beads on others.)

5. Students repeat Step 3, investigating how iodine solution can help them figure out the identity of their unknown powder. (Cornstarch, or any starchy powder, usually turns purple.)

6. If capable, students repeat Step 3, investigating what happens when each powder is heated. (Sugar usually melts. Citric or tartaric acid may brown, too.)

7. Classroom discussion prepares students for the final part of the investigation activity—figuring out the identity of an unknown powder.

8. Finally, students are ready to figure out the identity of an unknown powder, perhaps solving the puzzle with which the teacher began the activity. Students are given an unidentified powder, all the liquids and

materials they used in the previous six steps of the activity, and their notebooks, and told to try to figure out what powder they were given.

9. (Optional) By the time students are finished with this activity they will have had experience exploring and identifying properties of their powders, even if they have not formally been introduced to the concept. Now is an opportune time for the teacher to introduce the concept of properties, using students' various observations as examples. This would go a long way toward helping students understand performance expectation 5-PS1-3.

What's Happening? Powders can be identified on the basis of their unique chemical and physical properties.

NGSS Connections: Performance expectation 5-PS1-3 says students who demonstrate understanding can make observations and measurements to identify materials based on their properties. In this case, the materials they are identifying are the five (or six) white powders, and the properties they are using include their appearance, texture, and reactions to various liquids, heat, etc.

TRY IT!

As with other investigation activities in this book, Mystery Powders incorporates elements of the 5E or learning-cycle model of instruction. Setting the activity up in Step 1 is *engaging,* and all the steps that follow where students explore how their powders look, smell, feel, how they react to various liquids, and heat, are all *exploratory.* If the teacher uses the investigations as a way to formally introduce students to the idea of chemical or physical properties, then that serves as content introduction, or the *explanation* phase. Using learning to figure out contents of an unknown powder requires applying the new learning, the *expansion* phase of the 5E.

This investigation activity takes more time than others in this book. As such, I have known teachers whose students completed the Mystery Powders investigation activity early in a chemistry unit, and then in the weeks or months following the teachers referred back to students' experiences as examples of various other chemistry-related ideas being introduced. In this way, the entire investigation activity—all its steps—served as an exploration providing students with relevant, concrete background experiences related to later ideas. The approach applies some of the basic ideas about learning I discussed earlier in this book.

TEACHING TIPS

Step 1: Teachers often begin the activity by verbally or even physically setting up a hypothetical scenario, perhaps the story of a crime scene of some sort requiring identification of an unknown powder. You are almost certainly more creative than me; I leave the optional story creation to you. *Mystery Powders* is a popular investigation activity, however; the Internet will provide you with all sorts of tips, tweaks, and ideas about the activity.

Step 2: As students observe powders, the teacher can make statements or ask helpful open-ended questions like

- Tell me about what you're observing, followed by
- Are other powders the same? or
- Did you make the same observations about any other powders?

The teacher can help students recognize the importance (in the activity) of unique observations about any of the powders. People often note the smell of talc and the cube shape of salt crystals when magnified. Your students may note other things, too. That's part of the fun of open-ended activities!

Step 3: Results are written in notebooks; teachers may choose to discuss results as a class (or have students share by jotting observations on sticky notes) before continuing.

Students usually note vinegar produces fizzing when combined with baking soda, but none of the other powders. This is very helpful for determining whether the unknown (or "mystery") powder is or is not baking soda. If a "mystery" powder fizzes when vinegar is dropped on top, you have evidence the powder might be baking soda. On the other hand, if you do *not* observe fizzing you have evidence the powder is *not* baking soda.

Step 4: Students may note how some powders readily absorb water, and the water seems to bead (not be absorbed) on other powders. Some observations students make with vinegar and iodine solutions are actually from the water in the solutions; this step provides comparison data.

Step 5: Iodine is readily available to everyone in drugstores. You may decide you wish to do iodine testing as a teacher demonstration. A little extra care is needed with iodine because the solution can stain, and it's a poison if consumed in large volumes. Your students, however, will just be using a few drops at a time.

Students usually note iodine produces a dark color change in cornstarch (and flour), but none of the other powders.

Step 6: Powders can be heated over tea lights. I put a little powder on a piece of aluminum foil and hold the foil over the tea light's flame using a clothes pin. I wondered whether teachers felt small flames would be too dangerous for middle school students, so I asked a middle school teacher colleague familiar with the investigation activity about this, and she told me

> As for holding a piece of aluminum over a tea light, I would set up an apparatus for them. You can use a ring stand with a clamp to hold the foil and place the tea light beneath it. Or what I use to do when . . . we heated a great deal of water . . . was to set up a stand with two bricks. The bricks have enough space between them to place the tea light and then the aluminum container was placed on top. This keeps the students from accidentally dropping the aluminum and powder into the flame. If you place three or four tea lights in a row between the bricks, they can heat several powders at once, and they will all be the same distance from the flame. A good way to control that variable.

Alternatively, as with iodine, the teacher can heat each powder individually as a demonstration. Sugar melts and, if enough heat is supplied, chars and changes color (a process also called caramelization).

After Step 6, Before Step 7: Optionally, if citric or tartaric acid is one of the white powders being investigated, students can also examine what happens when a baking soda solution (baking soda dissolved in water) is dropped onto each powder. The combination usually fizzes.

Step 7: The teacher should ask students how they can tell whether each of the powders is the unknown, asking what evidence would tell them the powder was salt, sugar, etc.? Gathering, recording, and comparing responses helps ensure all students have ways to test the presence of any of the powders, setting them up for success, but students will not necessarily identify each substance the same way. That's OK. In fact, it's part of how science works. I note, for example, some students observe salt having a unique scent, others do not.

Step 8: I would suggest the teacher instruct students to write what they did, what they found, and what they were thinking as a result, that is, their procedures, data, and reasoning. To find out if they were "right," students can compare their results with those of their classmates trying to figure out which powder (of those they've tested) is being identified, probably discussing any differences. To encourage scientific argumentation, the teacher might suggest students use the phrase "I think the powder was _____ because _____."

If students have succeeded at identifying individual unknown powders, they could try identifying the contents of more sophisticated mixtures—those containing two or more powders. In addition, variations exist for this activity with powders in addition to the five I used in this example.

WHAT'S GOING ON IN THE SCIENCE?

Mystery Powders illustrates chemistry-related phenomena. Students see physical properties when they watch liquids be absorbed or not absorbed with water, or notice how salt crystals are always shaped like cubes. They observe chemical reactions whenever they see a color change or fizzing after a powder and liquid are mixed together. (The color change indicates a new substance has been produced, as does fizzing, which indicates the new substance is a gas.) Baking soda and vinegar, one of the combinations students observe, is the basis for the famous elementary school "volcano" to which you are, undoubtedly, familiar. And cornstarch mixed with water, another of the combinations students observe, is the recipe for "oobleck," also popular in elementary schools.

PRACTICES IN PRACTICE

NGSS's authors specifically mention the science and engineering practice of planning and carrying out investigations in conjunction with PE 5-PS1-3, pointing to the *Science Framework* stating students should be learning to

> Make observations and measurements to produce data to serve as the basis for evidence for an explanation of a phenomenon

NGSS Connection:
SEP3 Planning
and carrying out
investigations

Students are clearly planning and carrying out investigations anytime they are engaged in guided inquiry activities, including *Mystery Powders*. Science and engineering practices, however, are never practiced or applied in isolation from one another when scientific investigations are being done. In this activity students are also

NGSS Connection:
SEP1 Asking
questions and
defining problems

- *asking (implied) investigable questions* (SEP1) every time they say "I wonder if my unknown is . . . " Teachers teach the idea when they remind students the way to attempt to answer their questions is via investigation rather than, say, just asking the teacher "What powder is this?"

NGSS Connection:
SEP4 Analyzing
and interpreting
data

- *analyzing and interpreting data* (SEP4) every time they deduce the identity of an unknown. Teachers can help students learn this by asking how they know whether or not they are "right," and pointing out how scientists go through the same processes in their work.

NGSS Connection:
SEP7 Engaging in
argument from
evidence

- *engaging in argument from evidence* (SEP7) every time they use data to show classmates why they do or do not agree with their conclusions. Teachers reinforce this point by telling students scientists try to convince each other of ideas all the time, and using data or evidence is the most important tool they use to try swaying colleagues' conclusions. (Lee, Cite, & Hanuscin discuss this with a version of Mystery Powders featured in a 2014 *Science and Children* article.)

NGSS Connection:
Scientists use a
variety of methods.

CONNECTIONS TO THE NATURE OF SCIENCE

It is in the procedure's Step 7 where students are most strongly using deductive reasoning, one of science's methods, when figuring out the identity of unknown powders. If a student noted, for example, that cornstarch (and only cornstarch) created something purple when mixed with iodine solution, then she might use this deductive train of reasoning when testing an unknown powder:

IF only cornstarch looks purple when mixed with iodine,

AND my unknown looks purple when mixed with iodine,

THEN my unknown is cornstarch.

Or the converse:

IF only cornstarch looks purple when mixed with iodine,

AND my unknown does NOT look purple when mixed with iodine,

THEN my unknown is NOT cornstarch.

Similar reasoning applies throughout Step 7. Students are essentially making and testing predictions via a process of deductive reasoning. "Ooh, I think it might be salt!" exclaims a student. "Let's look at it in a magnifying glass! If I'm right, it'll look like little squares." That's equivalent to saying, "IF only salt looks like little squares, AND my unknown looks like little squares, THEN my unknown is salt."

THE PROBLEM WITH DEDUCTIVE REASONING

Deductive reasoning, like inductive reasoning, has its strengths and weaknesses. An investigation can ultimately *disprove* one or both premises of a deductive argument (the premises are the "IF" and "AND" statements in my examples, and the "THEN" statement is the conclusion). Investigations, however, cannot *prove* premises are *true*. If I gave you a white powder you've never seen before—something other than the five or six mystery powders— and you found it turned purple with iodine you have not proven the powder is cornstarch. Perhaps other powders you don't know about also turn purple with iodine. There's no way for you to know with complete certainty.

If the *premises* are true, then the conclusion will also be true. But the chain of reasoning does not work backwards. A *conclusion* that is true, by itself, does not prove the premises were true.

This point is important because this kind of deductive process is how explanations and other theory-like ideas are tested in science. It's all about predictions. A scientist reasons, "if my explanation is accurate, and I perform a particular investigation, then I expect a particular set of results." The student says "if my powder is baking soda, and I drop vinegar on it, then I expect to see fizzing." And the chemist says, "if mass is conserved in a chemical reaction, and I perform an experiment where I cause a reaction to happen inside a tightly sealed container, then I expect the container's mass won't change."

An explanation that accurately predicts the result of an investigation has not necessarily been proven correct. Other explanations may also predict results. If the Earth stood still, for example, and the rest of the universe revolved around it, and if I watched the stars for several hours, then I would predict they would move in a circular path above my head. The observation that this is what happens does not prove the Earth is the center of the universe!

CONCLUSION

Scientists—and students—often use inductive reasoning when finding patterns in data and generating scientific laws. They use deductive reasoning when testing explanations and scientific theories. The processes work together, complementing one another, to create the rich, useful description of nature that science provides. As noted in the *Science Framework* earlier in this chapter, it's more complex, but more rewarding, than the simplistic "scientific method" promulgated in textbooks and science classes. It's a point the *Framework's* authors repeated again

> A focus on practices (in the plural) avoids the mistaken impression that there is one distinctive approach common to all science—a single "scientific method." (p. 48)

and again

> Practices are defined as meaningful practices in which learners are engaged in building, refining, and applying scientific knowledge to understand the world, and not as rote procedures or a ritualized "scientific method." (p. 254)

Additional Resources

To learn more about sinking and floating, see www.nsta.org/pub lications/news/story.aspx?id=50932 for information about an activity like the one I described, and a follow-up examining sinking, floating, and density. In addition, Vincent, D., Cassel, D., & Milligan, J. (2008, Feb). Will it float? A learning cycle investigation of mass and volume. *Science and Children, 45*(6), 36–39 describes a 5E model lesson appropriate for students in Grade 5 and higher.

To explore the clay boat extension investigation activity further, see www.teachengineering.org/activities/view/duk_float_mary_act.

To learn more about mystery powders, see Kotar, M. (1989, March). Demystifying mystery powders. *Science and Children, 26*(6), 25–28 and Lee, E. J., Cite, S., & Hanuscin, D. (2014, September). Taking the "mystery" out of argumentation. *Science and Children, 52*(1), 46–52 as well as Mystery Powders: An introduction to physical and chemical properties. Retrieved from http://serc.carleton.edu/sp/mnstep/activities/26786.html. Many additional Web resources are available simply by searching "mystery powders lab" to learn more.

To learn more about how science works differently than portrayed by a simple five-step method, see the Understanding Science website (undsci.berkely.edu), especially the "How Science Works" section (undsci.berkely.edu/article/howscienceworks_01).

Chapter 5

I Must Be a Bit Indirect in This Chapter

Why is indirect evidence important to science?

In this section, you will come to see how

- indirect evidence plays a vital role in many science disciplines;
- assumptions underlie all scientific investigations; and
- observation is subjective; it depends on the observer's pre-existing knowledge and views.

You will be able to

- help your students understand how scientists can know about phenomena they can't witness.

Anyone teaching or learning about science will someday be asked, "How can they know what animals did millions of years ago if no one was around to see them?" Or maybe, "How can they know about stars thousands of light years away? No one can go there!" These are legitimate questions; you may have even asked them yourself. They are part of understanding how science works.

The questions relate to the nature of evidence. As discussed in earlier chapters, scientific knowledge is based on empirical evidence, but what "counts" as (empirical) evidence? Questions like those in the previous paragraph imply that only evidence from direct observation matters in science. Critics claim anything else is mere speculation. That's a misconception.

INDIRECT EVIDENCE

Scientists pay attention to another kind of evidence. On TV crime shows, the heroic detectives and forensic science experts go to crime scenes, collect hair, fibers, and other evidence, which they take to the lab. Moments later the quirky lab technician tells us DNA testing shows that the hair sample was from John Q Badguy, and fibers they collected and footprints they found indicate he was hiking last week in the Great Smoky Mountains wearing new work boots.

Although savvy viewers recognize lab tests take more than 30 seconds, most of us accept the basic premises behind the tests. If a piece of hair with someone's DNA is found in a room, we accept the conclusion he or she was *probably* in the room. Have we *proven* the person was in the room? Not necessarily; science does not prove most conclusions. We do, however, feel confident about our inferences—much like jury members can agree at a level beyond "reasonable doubt." If the person's wallet is also found in the room, we feel even more confident the person was there. A faded looking receipt in the wallet dated April 11 supports the conclusion the person was in the room after April 11.

Indirect evidence is evidence establishing a conclusion when combined with one or more inferences; also called circumstantial evidence. Evidence other than direct eyewitness observations is considered indirect.

These conclusions are made even though no one *saw* the person in the room. The hair, the wallet, and the receipt at a crime scene are all ***indirect evidence*** of the person's presence in the room.

If you decided to teach Mystery Powders from the last chapter by first creating a story about a crime scene with white powders left behind, you associated each powder with a suspect, and you had students analyze the powders to figure out which suspect most likely committed the crime. You and your students were using this same kind of reasoning.

In fact, your students may have used reasoning based on indirect evidence before the investigation activity even started. Perhaps they walked into your classroom, saw sets of hands-on materials distributed around the room, and became excited. They inferred they were going to do a science activity. They knew this even though they *did not see you setting up the activity*, and *did not hear you tell them they were going to be doing it*. Indirect evidence!

So, how can "they" know about dinosaurs or stars if no one was there to see them? The same way they know who the murderer was on NCIS/CSI/SVU: indirect evidence.

To illustrate the concept in a classroom, consider an activity designed to help students learn about animals scientists classify as carnivores, herbivores, and optionally omnivores.

Identifying Carnivores and Herbivores by Their Skulls

Overview: Students identify common features of carnivore, herbivore, and optionally, omnivore skulls, then apply this learning to dinosaurs.

Grades: Fourth grade or higher

Time needed: 30–60 minutes

MATERIALS

- Students will need to see pictures or hold models of herbivore and carnivore skulls.

INSTRUCTIONS

1. Teach students the definitions and distinctions between the words *carnivore* and *herbivore*. This introductory part of the lesson should be fast, simple, and refer to example animals familiar to students.

2. Hand out or show students photos (or models) of carnivore and herbivore skulls.

3. Students brainstorm differences they observe between the two groups. Try to create a class list of key differences observed.

4. Once the class agrees on ways carnivore and herbivore skulls look different, the lesson continues with students testing their ideas by finding out whether they can predict if photos of *other* animal skulls come from carnivores or herbivores.

5. Finally, the activity concludes with students predicting whether they think particular dinosaurs or extinct animals were probably carnivores or herbivores and communicating the evidence they believe supports their conclusions. The general procedure is similar to the previous part of the activity. Students examine photos (or models) of dinosaur skulls and try to figure out whether they believe the animals ate meat, plants, or both.

What's Happening? Carnivores (animals that eat other animals, predators), herbivores (animals that eat plants), and, optionally, omnivores (animals that eat meat and plants) can be identified by their skulls.

NGSS Connections: Performance expectation 4-LS1-1 says students who demonstrate understanding can construct an argument that plants and animals have internal and external structures that function to support survival, growth, behavior, and reproduction. (The features identifying carnivores and herbivores, related to killing, eating, or avoiding being eaten, all support survival and growth.)

TRY IT!

This investigation activity applies some of the principles behind the 5E or learning-cycle model of instruction, even though it's not a full-fledged 5E lesson. When students examine and brainstorm differences between carnivore and herbivore skulls (Steps 2 and 3), they are *exploring*. When the teacher helps students reach consensus views on how carnivore and herbivore skulls look different (Step 4), this is *explaining*. And when students go on to use their new learning to see if they can identify *other* carnivores and herbivores by their skulls' appearances (Step 4), as well as dinosaur skulls appearances (Step 5), they are using their learning in new contexts, the *elaboration* phase of the 5E or learning-cycle model.

TEACHING TIPS

Steps 2, 4, and 5: To do this lesson, students need to see and perhaps touch models of animal skulls. Holding a 3D representation of a skull permits a closer kind of observation than seeing a photograph. Obviously, photos are less expensive than 3D models. Photos are readily available online; try searching for images with phrases like "carnivore skulls" and "herbivore skulls" as a starting point.

If budgets prohibit individual or group copies of photographs, teachers can project images of multiple herbivores, that is, three to four herbivore skulls on a single slide, and three to four carnivores on a single slide. Projecting multiple images simultaneously is necessary so students can look for common features. Handouts permitting students to compare carnivore and herbivore skulls, however, looking for differences between the two groups, are even better.

Common herbivores include rabbits, deer, sheep, and cows. Common carnivores include dogs, cats, bobcats, badgers, and sea lions.

Common omnivores include bears, raccoons, coyotes, and humans. Omnivore skulls usually exhibit characteristics of both herbivores and carnivores. The differences between omnivores and the other classifications can be subtle, so distinguishing them can be more difficult than recognizing carnivores and herbivores. That's why I consider any parts of this lesson using omnivore skulls as optional.

Step 5: Finally, if the teacher is really into the topic, she might even tell students a little about other evidence supporting conclusions about what particular dinosaurs ate. To learn more, check out the resources listed at the end of the chapter.

WHAT'S GOING ON IN THE SCIENCE?

When people compare carnivore and herbivore skulls, differences in the animals' teeth, eyes, and jaws may be particularly notable.

FIGURE 5.1 Cat Skull

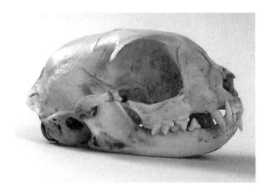

Image of a cat skull

FIGURE 5.2 Sheep Skull

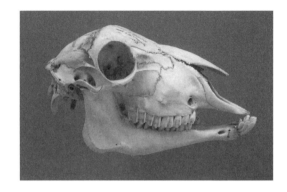

Image of a sheep skull

- Teeth are among the most commonly found fossils, probably because they are covered by strong, durable enamel more resistant to decomposition than other body parts. Carnivores generally have lots of sharp teeth (advantageous for tearing and cutting flesh), while herbivores have flatter teeth (advantageous for grinding nuts, berries, and other plant materials). Herbivores can have sharp teeth, too, but they don't usually have large, sharp canines (i.e, the two large teeth we associate with Dracula).
- An almost beak-like skull appearance that comes from a couple of teeth in the front of the skull, flat teeth in the back, and little bone in between, is characteristic of herbivores. A mouth full of sharp teeth is characteristic of carnivores.
- Carnivores usually have large, front-facing eyes (and eye sockets), while herbivores have eyes that face to the side. These adaptations help carnivores perceive depth (3D-vision), while herbivores can see a wider field of vision, helpful for spotting the carnivores that want to eat them.
- Students may also mention the animals' snouts (noses) and jaws. A large snout often implies the animal has a great sense of smell, but there are carnivores and herbivores with sensitive snouts so this may not always be a reliable way to differentiate between the two groups. Similarly, herbivores often have large jaw bones (providing lots of space for powerful chewing muscles to connect the jaws), but sometimes carnivores have powerful jaws too.

FIGURE 5.3 Triceratops Skull

Image of a Triceratops skull

Scientists apply the same kind of thinking when examining dinosaur skulls. A skull like that of the *Triceratops*, for example, bears many similarities to that of modern herbivores. Students readily recognize *Triceratops* skulls look more like those of deer, cows, and other herbivores than those of carnivores like dogs and cats. With your guidance, students can state their thoughts as scientific arguments, for example, present a claim ("I think this skull is from a herbivore.") supported by evidence and reasoning ("It has flat teeth, eye holes on the sides of its head, and a big jaw bone. Herbivores we saw before also had flat teeth for grinding hard plants, wide-spaced eyes so the animals could see dangerous predators, and big jaws to hold strong chewing muscles.")

PRACTICES IN PRACTICE

At first blush this may not seem like a scientific investigation. However, your students really are using scientific practices during the activity:

NGSS Connection:
SEP4 Analyzing and interpreting data

- When students examine other skulls, finding out whether they can predict an animal's eating behaviors, they are *making predictions* ("I think this skull is from a carnivore.") and then *analyzing and interpreting data* (empirical data are used to determine whether initial predictions were supported). You can reinforce these points by saying things like "What do you predict?" and "Your prediction was supported."

NGSS Connection:
SEP7 Engaging in argument from evidence

- Similarly, when students are discussing amongst themselves, referring to photos or models and trying to convince others they are right, they are *engaging in argument from evidence*.

NGSS discusses age-related differences you may note when students are engaging in argument from evidence.

- **In the 3–5 classroom,** students can present evidence and reasoning supporting their ideas, respectfully critique others' thoughts, and distinguish facts, reasoned judgment based on findings, and even speculation based on explanations (NGSS Lead States, 2013a, p. 13).

- **In the 6–8 classroom,** students can present and critique ideas and the evidence and reasoning supporting the ideas, too. The way I interpret NGSS's Appendix F, the differences in these abilities between younger and older students are fairly subtle. Older children argue from evidence with a little more emphasis and ability in using relevant evidence, scientific reasoning, and working with models (or problem solutions, in the case of engineering problems).

Although I am not sure the point applies to this specific activity, I also interpret NGSS's Appendix F to mean older children are also expected to be more skilled than younger ones at distinguishing and judging *between* two or more arguments or explanations for the same phenomena. Appendix F states students in Grades 3–5 "Compare and refine arguments based on an evaluation of the evidence presented," while those in Grades 6–8 "Compare and critique two arguments on the same topic and analyze whether they emphasize similar or different evidence and/or interpretations of facts." (NGSS Lead States, 2013a, p. 13)

In terms of this last point, scientists are often faced with situations in which they have two or more explanations for the same observations. This goes back to the point I made in earlier chapters about how a correlation between variables does not necessarily mean one caused the other; other explanations may apply. Observing a link between highway noise and poor health, for example, scientists might argue noise causes poor sleep, which contributes to poor health, or they might argue people living near noisy highways tend to have other characteristics (unrelated to highways noise) contributing to poor health. These are, in other words, "two arguments on the same topic." Older children would be expected to be more skilled than younger ones at figuring out whether data support one argument more strongly than the other.

> **Key Takeaway**
>
> A correlation doesn't always mean a causal relationship exists.

In this investigation activity, as is true for every investigation activity, for students to recognize the connection between their work and that of scientists, you must help them explicitly to make the connections. Simply doing hands-on science activities is *not* sufficient. So use phrases like

> **Key Takeaway**
>
> Explicitly help students recognize the connection to what they're doing and what scientist do.

- "Do you predict this skull is from a herbivore or a carnivore? . . . Why do you think so?" (or even "What is your argument?")
- "How do you know . . . ?" "What evidence can you point to . . . ?"
- Periodically remind students how their activities parallel those of scientists with phrases like "scientists also make and then test predictions" or "scientific conclusions are always based on evidence."

CONNECTING TO THE NATURE OF SCIENCE

Ultimately, it is clear to both teachers and students examining a model or photograph of a dinosaur skull like *Triceratops* that the animal was more likely an herbivore than a carnivore . . . even though no one was around to watch it eat. The skull fossil is *indirect evidence* supporting the conclusion.

Accompanying the indirect evidence is an assumption that carnivores and herbivores had the same characteristics in the past as in the present. If herbivores have big flat molars they use for grinding nuts and seeds today, we assume they did millions of years in the past, too. Scientists assume nature's "rules" (scientific laws) are timeless.

NGSS Connection: Scientific knowledge is based on empirical evidence.

It's also worth noting that evidence like a skull is limited in the questions it can support. For example, we might ask questions about what the animal's skin looked like, or how well it could hear. A skull probably cannot provide much evidence to answer questions like those. Scientific questions are ultimately answered empirically, and if you don't have evidence to answer a question, then you can't answer it.

ASSUMPTIONS

Philosophers of science recognize that all scientific investigations—including this skull activity—have underlying assumptions, a point almost never discussed in school science. It's not a major part of K–8 science—but it's worthwhile for you to know as a knowledgeable teacher. Accepting an investigation's results implies accepting its assumptions. Often this is a no brainer . . . but not always.

In this case of our dinosaur skull investigation, everything hinges on the assumption that the "rules" (or laws) for how nature works are unchanged over time. If animals with flat teeth and wide-set eyes eat plant-based diets today, then they did so in the past too. The idea makes sense to me, as it does to most scientists. If, however, a person rejected this thought and believed instead that "rules" governing nature in the distant past differed from those today, then she might conceivably reject the evidence supporting the idea that our fossil model came from an herbivore.

NGSS's authors recognize the point in one of their eight key ideas about the nature of science, discussed in NGSS Appendix H: "Scientific Knowledge Assumes an Order and Consistency in Natural Systems." They, too, state the idea as an assumption underlying investigations. In the case of the skull activity, we're assuming a consistency across time. Scientists also assume consistencies across space—we expect nature to behave the same everywhere.

NGSS Connection: Scientific knowledge assumes an order and consistency in natural systems.

If balls roll down hills and vinegar and baking soda fizz in a classroom in the United States, we expect the objects to behave the same way everywhere else on Earth, and always have. Similarly, we assume light behaves the same way everywhere in the universe as it does on Earth; it's an important assumption astronomers make when making conclusions about what's happening in galaxies far, far away.

As with all things scientific, the more evidence supporting a conclusion or assumption, the more likely the scientific community is to accept it—even if the idea can never be conclusively proven (as is so often the case in science). In the case of assumptions about dinosaurs eating flesh and having sharp teeth and forward facing eyes (like predators today), the assumption is strengthened if

- other aspects of the animals skeletons are *also* similar to predators today, or if
- fossilized remains of dinosaur "poop" (called coprolites by the scientists who study them) contain small animal bones, or if
- animal bones or egg shells appear to be present near where the animal's stomach would be when examining a dinosaur excavation site.[1]

OBSERVATION IS NOT OBJECTIVE

Philosophers of science also present us with the more challenging idea that observations are never truly objective. The basic idea is that everything we observe is at least somewhat conditioned by what we already know and believe. Their point challenges classical images of science, with science and scientists portrayed as objective. (Modern philosophers still say science strives for objectivity; they simply claim complete objectivity is ultimately not possible.)

When a child looks at an X-ray film of a femur bone, she sees a thick white line with knobs on the end (if she knows what knobs are). If she knows her letters, maybe she would say the white part of the image looks like the letter "I." You and I, as scientifically literate adults, recognize a femur or thigh bone. We might be able to deduce whether the bone is from a right or left leg. A biologist might be able to see an X-ray and deduce what animal the bone is from. And a radiologist seeing the same X-ray film would not only know it was a human femur but, possibly, also the person's age and sex. Closer examination might even lead the radiologist to conclude the person broke his leg several years ago, while pointing at something on the X-ray that looks like a smudge to me but like a well healed fracture to the radiologist.

The child, adults, and radiologist observed the same item but "saw" different things. In a real sense, we observe with our brains more than eyes or ears. Professional musicians hear things I do not when we listen to the same symphony. Similarly, wine connoisseurs definitely taste things I do not when we sip the same liquid. Physical sensations are interpreted and given meaning in the brain.

So what does this have to do with our skull lesson? Think about how you or your students might observe a skull before and after this lesson. Before the lesson, perhaps the students recognize a skull. They've seen skulls on TV, movies, maybe visits to museums. They probably recognize skull features, too—holes where eyes would be, teeth, etc. After the lesson, however, they might "see" skulls differently. Where they once "saw" eyes, now they also see where the eyes are positioned on the skull (facing forward for carnivores, more sideways for herbivores). Where they once saw teeth, now they might more fully notice details about the teeth. The size and shape of jaw bones might be observed differently, too.

Key Takeaway

Observations are conditioned by what we already know and believe.

My point is that anyone gaining specialized knowledge and training will learn to observe differently. We see, hear, taste, touch, and smell with our senses. We observe (and interpret) with our brains. To philosophers of science, all observation at some level is interpretation.

AN EXAMPLE

This point (and a few others) are illustrated in the classroom with an activity taken from the ENSI website where students are asked to create stories explaining a series of checks. I have taught this activity to many teachers, and know about its use with high school students, but I am unsure whether it would be appropriate for most students in Grades 3–8. I present it for you; imagine you are in a setting like a professional development workshop rather than your classroom.

The activity starts with participants being given an envelope containing several (fake) checks (see Figure 5.4). Small groups are instructed to take out three checks and create a story explaining the checks they see. After a little time for examining, discussing stories, and sharing results with classmates, participants repeat the process after removing three more checks—changing stories, as needed, now that six checks are being examined. Finally, participants remove three more checks from their envelopes and create one final story, based on the "data" from nine checks.

Stories vary, of course, and change as more checks are examined—just as scientific knowledge is open to revision in light of new knowledge—but the vast majority of adults I've worked with explain their check "data" by arguing that a couple named Paul and Leslie Millbank, whom they believe to be a husband and wife, had a daughter. At some later point in their lives, students usually say, Paul and Leslie divorced (supported by evidence about changes to the last names and addresses written on the checks). Explanations for why they divorced vary. (And the recognition the same check "data" can be explained multiple ways goes back to my previous point about arguing from evidence.)

NGSS Connection: Scientific knowledge is open to revision in light of new evidence. —NGSS Appendix H

FIGURE 5.4 Sample Checks

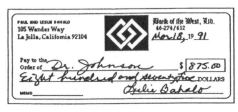

(Continued)

CHAPTER 5 • I MUST BE A BIT INDIRECT IN THIS CHAPTER

81

FIGURE 5.4 (Continued)

Sample checks from Check Activity.

The activity illustrates several aspects of the nature of science, including the points I made earlier about indirect evidence, assumptions, and subjectivity in observation.

- Everything we know about Paul and Leslie comes from their checks, not from observing them in person—indirect evidence.

- Most students immediately order the checks by date. They are familiar with the idea of a check, they know people date their checks when written, and know dates are placed in the upper right corner of each check. Someone who had never seen a check before might not react similarly. The things we already know—our preconceived ideas, knowledge, and experience—affect how we observe. In this way, observation is subjective.

- Similarly, one of the checks is marked as being to "NOW." Student interpretations of their check "data," and accompanying explanatory stories, differ depending on whether or not they interpret "NOW" as standing for the National Organization of Women. Everyone is technically seeing or observing the same checks, but the meaning they make varies depending on their preexisting knowledge and beliefs.

When philosophers discuss paradigms or theory-laden ideas they also often mention cultural aspects of science. The way a community of scientists thinks about science and what they do—science as seen from a sociological perspective—is part of a discipline's paradigm (at least the cultural aspects that are non-controversial and universally accepted). Many of my students will see a check to "Bunny's Ballet Studio" (dated several years after the students believe Paul and Leslie had a baby) and conclude the child is a girl. They do not picture a boy at a ballet studio. They are interpreting their data through their own lenses.

Are students 100% certain the child is a girl? No, especially after I note some boys like ballet and a place called a ballet studio may teach children other types of dance, too. They may feel "the evidence supports" their conclusion, or makes their conclusion "likely," but most recognize a single check to a ballet studio has not *proven* Paul and Leslie had a daughter.

With the available data—all of which is indirect evidence—no conclusion is certain. Science rarely proves anything. Nevertheless, some explanations are considered by students much more likely than others, mimicking the way the scientific community operates. I propose, for example, references to Paul and Leslie Millbank as a brother and sister, or even two men. I am generally unable to sway the class (the "scientific community") that I am right. This illustrates how scientific conclusions are not considered correct just because an authority figure says so (or it illustrates that I am not an authority figure).

Still, no one feels the evidence is sufficient, at any point in the activity, to say a particular explanation has been proven. Instead, claims can be made that the explanation Paul and Leslie are husband and wife have stronger evidence and are therefore more likely than alternatives. Scientists present explanations considered more (or less) probable than alternatives—but science can never absolutely prove anything with 100% certainty (see, for example, earlier discussions about how neither inductive nor deductive reasoning provides absolute proof).

One of the checks I usually draw students' attention to is made out to "Chevron." Students strain to find a way to fit this check into their explanatory stories. Personally, I do not think the check has anything important to do with a story about Paul, Leslie, etc. other than, perhaps, evidence they had a car. And that illustrates another point about what science is and how science works. Scientific conclusions, whether theory or law-like, are abstractions. Sometimes data neither support nor refute a conclusion and, in creating generalizations, can just be ignored. (Later scientists may interpret the same data differently, that's part of science, too.)

This point is usually missing from school portrayals of science, even during laboratory

> **Key Takeaway**
>
> Scientific conclusions are abstractions. Not all data are relevant, and scientists may interpret the same data differently.

activities. In typical school science labs, all data collected are expected to have a significance, to play a role toward an "expected" conclusion. Thus, students often believe any data not fitting the expectation are somehow "wrong," with the further implication the students themselves did something wrong. But, as illustrated by that Chevron check, that's not always the case. Sometimes nature is not as predictable as we wish it to be.

Finally, the ultimate question is what *really* happened with Paul, Leslie, and any children they might have had? And, just as is the case with real science, all we have is the evidence in front of us. No way exists to know with certainty—there are no answers in the back of the book of nature. Science is a social activity, a human endeavor, and so the best answer—for now— will be whatever the community of scientists decides. With students acting as scientists, they communicate with each other, share their thoughts and "data" to try convincing colleagues of a particular viewpoint, and when the dust settles, the best answer is the one most accepted by the community. The stronger the evidence, the more confident the community will be a particular conclusion is accurate. And if new information, or new ways of thinking about the existing information comes along, the community might shift its thinking. Its conclusions are open to revision—just like real science.

Case in Point

Indirect Evidence, Assumptions, and Subjective Observation in Real Science

Meet Lora Stevens, a colleague of mine in the Geology Department. Lora traces her interest in science to a teacher who took students to national parks to learn about geology—and have fun. Apparently the teacher was successful because today she's a geologist specializing in paleoclimatology—the study of ancient climates.

Until we can travel back in time, no one will be able to directly observe the weather thousands of years ago. So how in the world can paleoclimatologists study something like that? As with our skulls and checks, it's ultimately all about indirect evidence.

As an example, she told me about a project she began soon after completing her Ph.D. Her dissertation advisor had data about pollen (or seeds) in a sample of ancient mud—10,000-year-old mud core samples from present-day Iran. (Scientists knew about the mud's age via radiocarbon dating.) Scientists are interested in ancient mud because they are curious about when people started growing wheat and cultivating plants—essentially, when nomadic hunting and gathering people started to stay in one place. Anthropologists believe this development freed people from the need to constantly be looking for food, and was an important precursor to the development of written language, mathematics, and other hallmarks of what we often call "civilization."

Scientists closely examine ancient soil samples for clues about what was alive at the time. If a mud sample is filled with grass seeds, scientists conclude indirect evidence supports the idea there was a lot of grass in Iran at the time. And if the sample contains no seeds (or pollen) from any kind of tree, the scientists conclude the area was not forested at the time. The data do not *prove* anything, but they provide clues making particular conclusions more or less likely. The more data from different sources supporting a conclusion, the more confident the scientific community is that the conclusion is "true."

When Lora started this project, scientists already had indirect evidence indicating different plants were present in the area 10,000 years ago than today. When they examined mud samples they mostly saw pollen from grasses, so they believed the area was predominantly grasslands; the same area today is covered by trees. Other data indicated a transition from grassland to forest was due to local climate changes, like changes in rainfall. Lora, however, was interested in more precisely understanding how and when the climate in the area changed.

She had her own ideas, believing the area experienced many short, intense periods of drought. Science, however, is not merely about opinions. Science demands evidence. Ideas are no stronger than the evidence supporting them. She began the project firmly expecting evidence confirming her thoughts; other data already supported the idea that conditions in the area were generally dry, and her predictions meshed with the generally accepted ideas.

Other researchers had examined pollen *inside* the mud, but newer technology allowed her to examine the mud *itself* for climate clues. In other words, she could examine the same mud samples as others, but do so in a different way and learn different things about the climate. The newer chemical techniques, she believed, would allow her to draw more fine-grained conclusions about past climate in the area than previous techniques.

But she was wrong. The data that emerged were unexpected. In fact, they were downright confusing.

She had hoped and expected her chemical data would add details about the same conclusions as previous pollen data—the past was drier than the present in this part of the world. Her data, however, said the exact opposite. Her data indicated the area was *wetter* in the past.

What is a scientific researcher to do at this point? Flip a coin? Pick a favorite conclusion and just go with it, ignoring contradictory evidence? No, of course not; that's not how science works. Scientific conclusions need data support. The more data supporting a conclusion, the more likely the community of scientists is to accept it. And in this case, there wasn't enough data to support *any* conclusion. (Or you could say different data supported contradictory conclusions.)

Lora was faced with two explanations, two stories about the past that seemed equally plausible. More data were needed. But there wasn't any.

So she decided to take a closer look at the data she had. Remember how I said observation is somewhat subjective, how it depends on what the observer already knows? Faced with new possibilities, new ways of thinking, she reexamined her evidence. Evidence and its explanation are separate entities; the same evidence might be explained multiple ways. So she mentally experimented with different models, different explanations, to see if there was any way *all* the data could support just one of the competing conclusions.

And she found one.

All scientific investigations have underlying assumptions, as I discussed earlier in this chapter. Lora found that if she changed one of those assumptions, she could interpret all the data to support the idea that conditions were drier in the past. To accept her reinterpretation, one had to accept that 10,000 years ago, in Iran, for awhile, it rained only in the winter, not in the summer.

When I pointed out this was the conclusion she'd originally hoped to find, Lora agreed, but said the reinterpretation was not just a reiteration of her hopes. "There is," she said, "no robust data that support hope." How then can a scientist like Dr. Stevens convince colleagues to accept her new assumption? Science, after all, is a social activity; work is only "true" when accepted by the scientific community.

She published her findings in a scientific paper. Clearly and cleanly presenting her data, with all its contradictions, she laid out her interpretation—including the new assumption. She made her point: accept the assumption and the two datasets could agree; reject the assumption and the datasets conflict with one another. And then she waited for her peers' reactions.

This is the moment in a movie where the heroic scientist's work is accepted, her efforts are vindicated, and once-doubting colleagues grudgingly salute her accomplishments. But life is not a movie. Scientists are not so easily swayed to conclusions. Instead they said "interesting idea . . . but we're still not convinced, one way or another."

Papers are presented but, in real life, scientific investigations don't really end. They change, they go in new directions, but they keep going. One investigation raises questions and ideas leading naturally to new investigations. And that was the case here.

Lora's assumption about rainfall was radically different than generally accepted, and it generated new questions, new ways of thinking—and new searches for data. New studies and new datasets followed. The question is still not settled, but for Lora—and several colleagues around the globe—a whole new line of research began.

How will she know if she's right? Lora tells me data are actually starting to emerge indicating she was wrong. When will she know for sure? "We won't," she told me. "We never do. And that's frustrating. We never have certainty." Indeed, one of science's hallmarks is the tentativeness of its knowledge; sometimes scientific knowledge changes. The accumulation of evidence supporting some ideas is so massive they are unlikely to change. Nevertheless, anyone doing science (especially cutting edge work) must accept that ideas we hold near and dear can change tomorrow.

This work, however, is still the work she is most proud of, because it sparked a whole new line of research. "We are constantly looking at our datasets, asking if we interpreted them right. Sometimes we get new data, different ways of thinking about things. . . . And it changes everything."

CONCLUSION

Sometimes science is portrayed as a process of meticulous, careful observation by very smart, objective, logical people. Scientists often strive to emulate this ideal. However, neither science nor scientists always act this way. Observation is always filtered through our preexisting knowledge and beliefs, and assumptions underlie all investigations. In some sense, all observation is inference. There's a subjective element to science.

This is part of what makes science so interesting. Scientists create, discuss, argue, and persuade each other, while interpreting their carefully made inferences. It's more than just opinions—we always ultimately refer to evidence, for example, and conclusions generally need to jibe with a field's accepted ideas—but it's also a human process. We're not robots, after all; we are living, breathing people trying our best to interpret the observable world.

Additional Resources

A child friendly introduction to carnivore and herbivore skulls can be retrieved from. www.lakesidenaturecenter.org/AOM%20-%20 General%20-%20Mammal%20Skulls%20and%20Teeth.pdf. See http:// scienceline.ucsb.edu/getkey.php?key=198 and associated links for more detailed information. And see http://seplessons.ucsf.edu/

(Continued)

(Continued)

node/366 for directions and further information about a slightly different version of this lesson.

For the check activity, see Loundagin (1996) on the Web at www.indiana.edu/~ensiweb/lessons/chec.lab.html for information about the activity and copies of all necessary materials. I use the checks listed as a "second version," contributed by Leslie Hays and Paul Loozen. The ENSI website includes alternative activities, some of which might be appropriate for middle school children. The activity was also discussed at http://serc.carleton.edu/teacherprep/resources/activities/ordeal.html, and there's an online version at www.pbs.org/wgbh/evolution/educators/course/session1/explore_a.html.

NOTES

1. Recognizing assumptions are part of all scientific investigations makes this a good place to mention the work of a philosopher named Thomas Kuhn. Kuhn wrote an influential book in the early 1960s called *The Structure of Scientific Revolutions,* which impacted how people thought about the nature of science. Kuhn's work probably has a fairly minor impact on the picture of science portrayed in NGSS, but it was enormously influential to modern views on the nature of science.

   The assumptions we all accept are part of the current paradigm, including the belief nature behaves the same way everywhere and always has. The way scientists typically think about problems is part of the paradigm. Everything we consider "normal" science is part of the current paradigm—including everything in NGSS and the Framework. In short, when we teach students science's content, practices, values, and ways of thinking about the world we are teaching them the currently accepted paradigm.

   Kuhn was interested in the rare times when big ideas in a discipline are replaced with radically different ones. In any given discipline, they probably happen once a century and literally change how scientists think about their disciplines. Plate tectonics was a revolutionary change in geology, as was astronomy's change from an earth-centered to sun-centered universe. Evolution (and its synthesis with genetics) was revolutionary to biology.

   Normally, when results do not fit the way scientists think about the world, the scientific community finds some way to accommodate them. Sometimes current ideas are tweaked. Other times, frankly, data or results are ignored or dismissed because they seem impossible or otherwise fly in the face of the established facts universally accepted as true. We tend to admire the scientists whose ideas were initially considered farfetched, but ultimately turned out to be "true," like Alfred Wegener and the idea that continents are moving, or the scientists hypothesizing tiny birds are descended from dinosaurs (which, by the way, is in turn based on assumptions about evolution in biology's current paradigm). Most of the time, however, ideas ignored or dismissed by the scientific community probably lack merit.

Every once in a great while, though, scientists will find problems where current thinking just does not work, or some seemingly farfetched idea might just work better to explain and predict. This could conceivably represent the start of a scientific revolution. They happen rarely, but they do happen.

Chapter 6

Scientists Do Experiments . . .

*What procedures do scientists use
when answering questions?*

In this section, you will come to see how

- scientists don't always answer questions via experiments, and
- different experimental designs have individual strengths and weaknesses.

You will be able to

- help your students explore nature in the schoolyard, performing a nonexperimental scientific investigation, and
- help your students begin thinking critically about variable control and investigation "fairness."

I n this chapter, we take a closer look at scientific investigations and how they work. I've used the word *investigation* throughout this book when discussing how scientists create or test ideas. Often we talk about experiments, however, as synonymous with investigations. After all, scientists do experiments, right?

NGSS Connection:
SEP3 Planning and carrying out investigations

Not necessarily.

Some science is *not* experimental. NGSS's authors recognize the point when titling Practice 3 "Planning and Carrying Out Investigations." We looked at some examples of investigations that were not classical experiments in the last chapter. In this chapter, we wade into the world of research design—a fancy way of saying "planning an investigation." The topic has implications for you as a 3–8 science teacher, but also as a citizen.

As a citizen you are bombarded with scientific information and discussions about studies (especially health-related studies). Moreover, as a teacher, you hear about educational research studies. How are you to be critical consumers of this information, deciding whether it's trustworthy? And how are you going to help your *students* become adults who are critical consumers of scientific information? Understanding research designs, including their strengths and weaknesses, goes a long way.

But let's start smaller. A lot smaller.

Investigating Pillbugs

Overview: Students explore the school grounds, noting where pillbugs are found.

Grades: Third or higher

Time needed: About 30 minutes

MATERIALS

- Small sticks or shovels for moving leaves and loose dirt (optional)
- Soap and water for cleanup
- Paper or notebooks for recording data about where pillbugs were found
- Small containers for storing pillbugs (optional)

INSTRUCTIONS

1. After being provided with minimal knowledge about where pillbugs typically live (under leaves or rocks, places that are dark and moist), students go outside and try to find pillbugs. Students can use things like popsicle sticks or small shovels to move leaves, twigs, etc. when searching for pillbugs; the idea is to be gentle so as to minimize chances of harming organisms—and maybe keeping hands, etc. clean.

2. When students find pillbugs, they should note where they were and what they observed about the pillbugs surroundings. Observations like these provide the beginning for students developing models about pillbugs and their habitats. They also provide the starting point for potential investigations to see whether (further) data support initial ideas.

FIGURE 6.1 Pillbug

Image of a pillbug

3. Students may, optionally, collect pillbugs, gently placing them in small containers and bringing them back to the classroom. (See Activity 7.)

What's Happening? Pillbugs are not insects, they breathe with gills. So they require moisture. That's why they typically live in dark, damp places like underneath leaves or rocks.

NGSS Connections: Disciplinary core idea LS2 is about ecosystems and ecology. Studying pillbugs and their environments plays a role toward helping children ultimately understand the performance expectations associated with this core idea. Performance expectation 3-LS2-1 says students who demonstrate an understanding can construct an argument that some animals form groups that help members survive. Performance expectation 5-LS2-1 says students who demonstrate understanding can develop a model to describe the movement of matter among plants, animals, decomposers, and the environment. And performance expectation MS-LS-2 says students who demonstrate understanding can construct an explanation that predicts patterns of interactions among organisms across multiple ecosystems.

TRY IT!

This investigation activity, on its own, is not a 5E or learning-cycle lesson. Students are, however, *exploring* to find out about where pillbugs typically live. As teacher, you decide how much information you want students to have before they begin searching for pillbugs, and how directive you feel the need to be regarding their observations. The best options will balance enough information so that students will find pillbugs, without being so directive or prescriptive as to take away the fun of discovery and the possibility of student-generated novel ideas. The ideas we tend to retain are those we create for ourselves, and having a tangible relevant experience before being introduced to new content enhances learning.

TEACHING TIPS

Look around the school grounds yourself ahead of time to make sure you know places where pillbugs are present. Damp, dark places are good starting points, like underneath leaf litter and near sprinkler heads. It may be a little easier to find pillbugs after a rain storm.

Step 2: If students work in pairs, one student can find the actual pillbugs, while the other records salient details in a notebook. This also provides an out for any student thinking pillbugs are just too yucky to be near.

Teachers can structure student observations, without being too directive, by having them write and make drawings about the conditions they observed around the pillbugs, and provide questions to cue thinking like

- What did you notice about where you found the pillbugs?
- Were the pillbugs someplace more wet or dry?
- Were they in sunlight or covered by shade?
- Would you say the pillbugs were more huddled together or spread out?
- Were other "bugs" around the pillbugs? If so, what did they look like?

Finally, you must also decide whether you want students to gently collect pillbugs to bring into the classroom for the other parts of the activity, or whether you would prefer to collect them yourself.

Pillbugs are also called roly poly "bugs" because when threatened, some varieties will roll into a protective ball shape. If children are gentle, they can pick up their pillbugs, whether rolled into a protective ball or not. Pillbugs can easily be coaxed into walking on a small stick or cotton swab, which can then be used to transfer them to a container. Pillbugs can safely be placed into just about any container. I usually (re)use inexpensive plastic Petri dishes.

WHAT'S GOING ON IN THE SCIENCE?

Although technically different, what I'm calling pillbugs are also called roly poly "bugs," sowbugs, isopods, doodle bugs, potato bugs, woodlice, and various other names. They are found just about everywhere—hence the wide variety of names—and children have been examining them in schools for years. If you live someplace with leaves falling off trees into the dirt, where it rains once in a while, you've probably got pillbugs running around somewhere. They are not insects and don't carry disease, bite, sting, fly, or jump. They have more in common with shrimp and crayfish than insects or other bugs. In fact, scientists classify them as crustaceans. They breathe through gills and require moisture and humidity to survive. As animals eating primarily fallen leaves and other detritus in the dirt, pillbugs are gentle creatures that play an important role in their ecosystems, essentially recycling matter.

Looking more closely at the investigation activity's NGSS-related core ideas, studying pillbugs, especially in the field, provides students with the chance to observe how they live and how they interact with their environment. This is ecology. The activity also provides a tangible, observable example of animals living in groups. The *Science Framework* points out, "Being part of a group helps animals obtain food, defend themselves, and cope with changes. Groups may serve different functions and vary dramatically in size." Pillbugs, living as a group, huddle together to share warmth and moisture, and they also share some resources. They preserve and conserve certain precious minerals in their diets, for example, by eating each other's poop.

I have a hunch students will remember that.

NGSS Connection:
SEP3 Planning and carrying out investigations

NGSS Connection:
Scientific investigations use a variety of methods.
—NGSS Appendix H

NGSS Connection:
SEP4 Analyzing and interpreting data

NGSS Connection:
SEP8 Obtaining, evaluating, and communicating information

NGSS Connection:
SEP7 Engaging in argument from evidence

PRACTICES IN PRACTICE

- As students are searching for and examining pillbugs in the wild, they are *planning and carrying out investigations*. The investigations *are not traditional experiments*, but the students *are* purposively collecting empirical data that help address questions about pillbug habitats.

- As students begin noticing patterns and developing tentative ideas about how and where pillbugs might live, they are simultaneously using multiple practices. They are *analyzing and interpreting data*, perhaps even *constructing explanations* or *developing models* about pillbug habitats. They may also be *obtaining, evaluating, and communicating information* and—as they discuss ideas amongst themselves—*engaging in argument from evidence.*

For instructional purposes, we try separating science and engineering practices into individual examples, places in investigations where students are applying a practice. In real science, though, sometimes the distinctions are subtle. Scientists—and students—often engage in more than one practice at a time.

As I've stressed throughout this book, simply engaging in these practices is necessary but not sufficient for student learning about the practices and developing accurate understandings of science's nature. To do this, the teacher can also ask questions like

- "What have we observed in our investigations?" (followed by accenting to students how they were doing investigations; perhaps also highlighting how scientists depend on observations as the basis for everything they do).
- "What do we think about pillbugs now that we've made these observations?" or "What are we thinking now about where pillbugs like to live?" (and then reinforcing scientists' conclusions are based on observations, or how scientists are always looking for patterns, too).

CONNECTING TO THE NATURE OF SCIENCE

Students exploring pillbugs in their natural habitats, creating ideas about where they "like" to live and what they eat, *are* doing science—even though they are not doing classical experiments. Scientific investigations aren't always classical experiments. Careful observation (guided by the observer's knowledge and beliefs) helps researchers generate ideas (hypotheses) worthy of further testing. That's an inductive process, generating new ideas. The additional testing could involve more observations in the field, perhaps even testing the extent to which laboratory-based conclusions are supported in real-life conditions. That's a deductive process, testing predictions.

Simply observing in real-life conditions, carefully and purposefully, help researchers understand *how* and *why* things are as they are.

Observing and investigating pillbugs in their natural habitats mimics this process, and presents an open-ended, exploratory activity to students. Students can further develop concepts about ecology and pillbug habitats when they examine the critters back in the classroom. And they can learn more about a different kind of scientific investigation—fair testing, or more classical experiments—while doing so!

Investigating Pillbugs
(continued)

Overview: Students design investigations to answer a question about pillbug preferences.

Grades: Third or higher

Time needed: 30–60 minutes

MATERIALS

- Pillbugs, probably collected on or near school grounds
- Petri dishes or similar small translucent containers
- Paper towels
- Water
- Magnifying glasses (optional)
- A small tub or similar container for keeping pillbugs in the classroom (optional)
- Keeping pillbugs alive in the classroom requires only small amounts of potato, carrot, or similar starchy vegetable, a few paper towels for the pillbugs to crawl under, and a spray bottle of water to keep them moist. (optional)

INSTRUCTIONS

1. Bring pillbugs into the classroom, ideally two or three for each student (though the investigations can be done with smaller number of critters). Students can bring pillbugs into the classroom, or you can collect a class set. You and your students will probably appreciate setting aside some time for students to simply observe the pillbugs (including, optionally, the use of magnifying glasses). Students' unstructured observations, along with your questioning about what students are noticing and thinking, may lead to a question for investigation in Step 2. Student enthusiasm here may increase the amount of time required for the activity.

2. Provide students with a question to answer experimentally, like "Do pillbugs prefer light or dark conditions?" (Alt: "Do pillbugs prefer wet or dry conditions?" or any other dual choice.)

3. Provide students with necessary materials and show them an experimental setup to address the question (basically, Petri dishes or preference chambers, pillbugs, and paper towels. The basic experimental procedure involves placing equal numbers of pillbugs in the two Petri dish chambers, covering one side with a paper towel, and waiting to see how many pillbugs end up in the darker and lighter sides of the Petri dish chambers. Usually, after a few minutes, most pillbugs have migrated to the darker side.

4. Lead a brief discussion about what students observed, accenting how their observations are *data*, and what is to be concluded from the observations. If students have previously been introduced to the concept of testable (or operational) questions, now might also be a time to reiterate the point.

5. However, discussion should soon focus on another question: What do we need to do to make sure this was a "fair test"?

6. Students can now go on to design their own fair tests to answer different questions they generate about pillbug behaviors and preferences (or, if necessary, revise and retry procedures to address the same question as earlier).

What's Happening? Pillbugs tend to congregate together, eventually. They need moisture to breath, and generally prefer environments that are darker or provide hiding places. They move more easily on some surfaces than others and usually cannot climb up walls.

NGSS Connections: Beside performance expectations mentioned for Activity 7, 3-LS4-3 says students who demonstrate understanding can construct an argument with evidence that in a particular habitat some organisms can survive well, some survive less well, and some cannot survive at all. The PE's clarification statement mentions the needs and characteristics of the organisms and their habitats.

In addition, performance expectation 2-LS2-1 says students who demonstrate understanding can plan and conduct an investigation to determine if plants need sunlight and water to grow, adding that assessment is limited to testing one variable at a time. Activity 7 has nothing to do with plants and sunlight, but applies the same principles of experimental design required in 2-LS2-1.

TRY IT!

Although students will undoubtedly learn about pillbug habitats and preferences, this investigation activity is more about students learning the concept of a "fair test" or controlled scientific investigation than anything else. It's not a 5E or learning cycle-based lesson, although students may be applying (or *expanding*) on their learning from Activity 7.

TEACHING TIPS

Step 1: I often find pillbugs for classroom use by making a simple pillbug "trap" out of a potato into which I carve tunnels or holes. I cut the potato in half, cut a couple holes or tunnels, and put it together with a rubber band so pillbugs have tunnels inside the potato to crawl in and out of. However, you may be able to attract the critters with nothing more than a few pieces of cut-up potato placed outside in an area where you've seen them before, for example, under leaf litter, near sprinkler heads, or anyplace dark and moist. I generally find lots of pillbugs in and around my potato after a day in a relatively dark, moist spot outdoors where pillbugs have been seen before. (See Reed [2016] for more details.)

I place the pillbugs in a small tub, where I can keep them alive as long as necessary. All they need to thrive is a place to "hide" (potting soil, leaf litter, or even just a wrinkly paper towel or two work well), a little moisture (a couple squirts with a water-filled spray bottle every day, a little more before the weekend), and a little bit of carrot or potato to eat. You can keep them covered with a loosely placed paper towel, to provide shade, if you like. People usually place a lid (with a couple of holes) over their pillbug "habitat," but even that is not strictly necessary since the pillbugs don't fly and can't crawl out of the container.

Worst case, pillbugs can be purchased from Carolina Biological Supply, though parents might also be able to find some for you at their homes.

FIGURE 6.2 Pillbug Preference Chamber

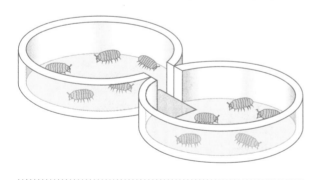

Pillbug Preference Chamber

Step 2: Once inside, students begin investigating pillbug behaviors using more formal experimental procedures, that is, fair testing. Students can brainstorm investigable questions (open inquiry) or you can provide specific questions you wish them to investigate (guided inquiry). Questions often involve pillbug preferences. Sometimes, however, teachers wish to lead an activity falling somewhere between guided and open inquiry.

Step 3: Preference chambers can be made by taping two Petri dishes together (in a figure-8 pattern), cutting away the dishes' sides where they meet. Pillbugs can then freely walk from one Petri dish to the other.

Step 5: The concept of a *fair test* is identical to that of controlling variables in designing classical experimental procedures. Students, assuming they are developmentally ready for this kind of cognitive activity, can begin identifying the sorts of things that would need to be kept the same for the pillbug test to be fair. "Things kept the same" are also known as experimentally controlled variables.

Fair test, or controlled scientific investigation, is one where the experimenter strives to keep all variables the same other than the one being investigated; differences in the dependent variable can be attributed to the independent variable.

In a fair test, there's only one difference between two or more groups being studied. If groups differ in more than one way (one variable), it's difficult to know which variable was responsible for any differences between the groups. For example, suppose you and your friends decided to lose weight by exercising, eating vegetables, and drinking water. A month later, you have all lost weight. Thinking like scientists, we can't really say whether the difference was due to the exercise, or dietary changes, or water consumption, or some combination of the three changes. On the other hand, if the only change you'd made was exercising more, and you all lost weight, you would be more confident the exercise was responsible for the differences you observed. The latter example represents a "fairer test," or a better-controlled scientific investigation.

To help wrap your head around this important idea, consider these examples for the question, "Do pillbugs prefer light or dark conditions?"

- Placing a bunch of pillbugs initially on both sides of an otherwise empty preference chamber—some on one side, some on the other side, covering one half of the chamber with a *damp, dripping* paper towel, and returning several minutes later to observe the pillbugs. (If the pillbugs end up on the darker side of the container, how do you know whether they were responding to the darkness or the moisture?)

- Placing all the pillbugs initially on one side of an otherwise empty preference chamber, covering that side of the chamber with a paper towel, and coming back several minutes later to find the pillbugs had not moved. Can you conclude pillbugs prefer darker environments? (How do you know the pillbugs might not *also* have remained stationary if you first put them in the uncovered, light side of the preference chamber? Maybe they're just not walking around in the conditions which you've placed them.)

- Placing two pillbugs initially on opposite side of an empty container, covering one but not the other with a paper towel, and coming back later to find both pillbugs under the paper towel. (Can you conclude pillbugs prefer darker environments? Maybe, but how do you know the one pillbug that moved to the darkness was a typical pillbug? Or the one pillbug that stayed in the darkness was typical, for that matter? It would be scientifically better to repeat the investigation with more pillbugs.)

PRACTICES IN PRACTICE

In this investigation activity, students plan and carry out their own investigations. When planning and carrying out investigations,

- **Students in Grades 3–5** should be learning about fair tests. They should also be making predictions about what they think will happen if a variable changes, which they then go on to test, perhaps with a little assistance from the teacher or peers.

- **Students in Grades 6–8,** on the other hand, are more sophisticated in their planning. They not only learn about fair tests—controlled scientific investigations—but they also learn to identify which variables represent their results, which are things they are intentionally changing from test to test, and which they need to keep the same (or control) across tests to help assure differences in their results can only be accounted for by differences in the things they intentionally changed from test to test.

In other words, older students are more sophisticated than younger students in their abilities to understand and discuss the importance of controlling variables in experimental procedures to increase the likelihood differences in dependent variables were caused by changes to independent variables. After conducting an investigation, older students can also start evaluating the procedures, thinking about how the procedures might have been changed to improve the investigation, or the accuracy of collected data.

In designing their own tests, students ultimately apply most NGSS science and engineering practices. For example,

- Students may be *asking (their own) questions and defining (their own) problems*, depending on how the teacher has set up the investigation activity. If students are given a question to investigate by the teacher, like whether pillbugs prefer light or dark conditions, they haven't actually asked their own questions—though you can still emphasize how scientists ask similar questions. If students are coming up with their own investigations, though, they are seeking answers to their own questions.

NGSS Connection:
SEP1 Asking questions and defining problems

- Student will be *planning and carrying out investigations*, perhaps beginning with pillbugs placed in a Petri dish with a paper towel in half the dish.

NGSS Connection: SEP3 Planning and carrying out investigations

- Upon completing investigations, students observing what happened amounts to *analyzing and interpreting data*.

NGSS Connection: SEP4 Analyzing and interpreting data

- They might be thinking about results, trying to figure out how or why pillbugs might behave as they do amounts to *constructing explanations* and maybe even *models* for pillbug behavior.

NGSS Connection: SEP6 Constructing explanations and designing solutions

- Of course, when students share their plans (or plans + data) with classmates, they might come to recognize "unfair" aspects to their experimental procedures. Students who want to test whether pillbugs prefer damp or dry conditions might put damp paper towels on the bottom of one side of a preference chamber and nothing on the other side, place pillbugs on both sides of the preference chamber, and observe where the pillbugs go. They might, however, later decide that maybe the pillbugs moved to the damp paper towel simply because they preferred walking on paper towels rather than uncovered Petri dish plastic. The students might decide their experimental procedure could be improved by accounting for this uncontrolled or confounding variable—going on to do it again, this time with damp paper towels in one half the container and dry (but otherwise identical) paper towels in the container's other half. The talking, discussing, and convincing students do in ultimately deciding to revise their procedures is probably *engaging in argument from evidence*. With this new procedure, the students would be able to argue (with evidence) more persuasively than before.

NGSS Connection: SEP7 Engaging in argument from evidence

CONNECTING TO THE NATURE OF SCIENCE

Students—especially younger children—are more likely to comprehend the idea of a fair test than that of controlling variables, although they are basically the same thing. In a fair test, everything that might affect the investigation's outcome is kept the same, except the factor the experimenter is trying to find out about. In our pillbug experiment, trying to find out whether pillbugs prefer light or dark, anything else that might affect where they voluntarily move should ideally be kept the same for all the pillbugs. So, if some pillbugs are initially put in the light and an equal number in the dark, the temperatures in the light and dark spaces are the same (otherwise you can't be certain whether you are measuring their light or temperature preferences), the moisture in the two spaces is the same (otherwise you can't be certain whether you are measuring their light or moisture preferences), the surface they walk on is the same (otherwise you can't be certain whether you are measuring their light or walking surface preferences), etc.

Controlled experimentation is part of classical science. One of this chapter's key takeaways is recognizing it's not the *only* part, but it's still an important part. Beginning with the concept of a "fair test," elementary teachers can provide students with experiences where they design and carry out experimental investigations. As students move to middle school, teacher-provided instruction about why tests are and are not fair help students eventually improve their abilities to recognize, design, and critique experimental investigations.

> **Key Takeaway**
>
> Controlled experimentation is an important part of classical science and can be introduced to even young children through the concept of a "fair test."

A SIDE-NOTE ABOUT EXPERIMENTAL RESEARCH DESIGN

The recognition that scientists use a variety of methods is the very first of NGSS's key understandings about the nature of science. I discussed it in chapter four—contrasting inductive and deductive methods—and other places in this book. Even within the seemingly specialized method of an experiment, scientists use varied methods. Planning and carrying out investigations is not always as simple and straightforward as portrayed, even with something as simple as an elementary student's science fair experiment or open-ended investigation activity.

As teachers, it's important for you to recognize this fact so that you will have a deeper, richer understanding than your students, but also as critical consumers of scientific and health information outside school, in your everyday life. Bombarded by studies, it's helpful to recognize different ways exist to examine a question and how to judge the trustworthiness of the information presented. To keep the examples familiar, though, consider a hypothetical science fair investigation: "Does the color of ink make a difference in how students do on multiple-choice quizzes?" I chose this example because it sounds like something a kid might investigate, but you can just as easily imagine an action research study of your own investigating whether some more sophisticated factor makes a difference in how students do on multiple-choice quizzes or any other educational outcome.

Do students writing with something other than black or dark blue ink perform differently than peers writing with other colors? Perhaps a student hypothesizes vibrant colors are distracting, and performance with them will decrease. Or maybe she believes they are easy to see and their vibrancy helps thinking, so performance will increase. (Data differ from their explanation; we might infer *multiple* ways to explain the same results.)

One way of doing this study is the kind of classical experiment I discussed with pillbugs in Activity 7, also called a ***randomized, controlled experiment.*** The student (with permission from the teacher) flips a coin at the beginning of a quiz, one flip for every student in the class. If the coin comes up heads, a student takes the quiz with a black pen. If the coin comes up tails, a student takes the quiz with a different color pen. (It's OK if the two groups are not exactly the same size.) The student would compare the average scores for students in the two groups. In the best of all cases the student would repeat the procedure, or gather data from multiple classes. In a randomized, controlled experiment, more is always better.

I will leave it up to you to think through factors that could and should be kept the same among the two groups for the experiment to be a fair test. This is the most important point to consider when evaluating a study.

A different way of experimentally investigating the question exists, however. ***Retrospective experiments*** (sometimes also called *case control experiments*) are common in health and education studies. Studies involving thousands of people usually follow this design.

A retrospective version of the study might begin with all the math quizzes taken by all the students in the school one week, grouped by those written in blue or black and those in a different color. Our student researcher would be given all the scores from both groups for comparison. The dataset would be much larger than for the other versions of the investigation. (Presumably, our student researcher would be given information without any attached names, for privacy purposes.) Our student could find out the averages for both groups.

Randomized, controlled experiment is one in which test subjects are randomly assigned to various treatment or control groups; random assignment minimizes preexisting differences among experimental groups. Ideally, the groups differ only in the independent variable controlled by the experimenter.

Retrospective experiment is one in which researchers begin with an effect and search backward in time to find potential causes, examining differences in subjects that did and did not exhibit the effect.

This study could be performed quickly—after all, the math quizzes have already been completed, graded, and recorded—but critical readers can probably find multiple ways to explain any group differences, and the differences may not reflect simple color preferences. If girls prefer brightly colored ink, for example, then the student might ultimately be studying performance of boys vs. girls more than anything else. Or if pens with brightly colored ink are expensive, perhaps the data reflect socioeconomic differences more than color preferences. Or if pens with brightly colored ink are hard to find, perhaps the data reflect parental involvement in their child's education, etc.

And then there's the issue of students using pencils. Should they simply be ignored? Or do they count as part of the black and blue group? Different answers to that question could lead to different results!

Each investigation has its advantages. The randomized, controlled experimental investigation is probably the best test from a scientific perspective—the groups being compared are likely to be similar since participants were randomly assigned. On the other hand, classmates may not love the idea of being forced to use a different pen than normal. Some might even refuse to participate. And teachers might decide forcing someone to use a different writing implement on a quiz that counts for a grade is unethical.

The retrospective version of this experimental investigation circumvents ethical considerations, is fast and easy, and would have a large dataset—decreasing the chances one or two students could act as outliers throwing off results. However, the likelihood the two groups compared were similar in every way except for pen color—that the comparison was fair—is much smaller than in the randomized experiment. Differences may reflect group differences other than ink color. Put another way, the results from this retrospective experimental investigation might tell us whether math scores differ for students using blue/black pens vs. other color pens, but the results would *not* tell us the differences were *caused* by the pens.

PRACTICES IN PRACTICE

Although the previous example was written with teachers in mind, your students also read and examine grade appropriate nonfiction text and other media (including tables, diagrams, and charts). SEP8 is *Obtaining, Evaluating, and Communicating Information*. It's an SEP concerned with students being critical consumers of scientific information. As a skilled elementary or middle school teacher, you are more skilled than I am at helping students develop critical reading and communication skills; it's part of subject areas in addition to science. However, NGSS can help guide you in figuring out grade level expectations for students at your school.

NGSS Connection:
SEP8 Obtaining, evaluating, and communicating information

In discussing SEP8 in Appendix F, the authors distinguish expectations for students in Grades 3–5 compared to those in Grades 6–8. The appendix notes that

- **students in Grades 3–5** reading grade-appropriate text (and other media) should ultimately be able to summarize their reading and obtain details, describe how the reading or details are supported by evidence, compare or combine their understandings across multiple texts or media, and explain phenomena, or provide solutions to a design problem. Older students can be more sophisticated in these abilities.

- **students in Grades 6–8** reading grade-appropriate text (and other media), including qualitative, quantitative, or technical info should ultimately move from summarizing to also figuring out central or key ideas in their readings, as well as moving from getting details to recognizing which details are specifically about researchers' results and conclusions. Older readers are more skilled than younger ones at critically evaluating what they read, assessing its credibility, even recognizing potential biases, as well as assessing how ideas are (or are not) supported by evidence.

This leads me to believe older students can begin critically evaluating articles and other discussions about scientific and health investigations of the sorts I discussed in this section.

CONCLUSION

Scientists perform all sorts of investigations, only some of which are true experiments with control and experimental groups. And even within this category, different types of experimental designs exist. Studies reported in the media often use retrospective-type designs. Critical consumers should look to see whether reports include discussion about efforts the researchers undertook to try to make the comparison groups as equivalent as possible (i.e., fair tests). Even then, we should be skeptical drawing conclusions about one factor *causing* another.

Additional Resources

To learn more about pillbugs, see Dobson, C., & Postema, D. (2014). The amazing ecology of terrestrial isopods. *Science and Children,* 51(7), 60–66. Morgan, E., & Ansberry, K. (2016, April/May). Roly-poly pillbugs. *Science and Children,* pp. 15–21 discusses K–2 and Grade 3–5 activities and trade books about pillbugs. Learn about how a teacher had students examine pillbugs at http://blog.growingwith science.com/2009/10/pill-bug-activities-for-kids/.

Learn more about fair testing at http://undsci.berkeley.edu/article/fair_tests_01.

Chapter 7

We're Counting on You

What do I need to know about data?

In this section, you will come to see how

- real data usually vary, adding an element of subjectivity to their analysis, and
- different kinds of numerical data have individual strengths and limitations.

You will be able to

- help your students recognize natural variation, and
- help your students understand the kinds of conclusions possible from different data types.

As laboratory activities become more open-ended and inquiry based—more like real-life science—the resulting data become "messier," more varied, and more in need of nuanced analysis and interpretation than data generated from contrived cookbook activities. But this is also one of the hallmarks separating real-life science investigations from the more traditional cookbook activities children are sometimes asked to do in school. In fact, it's fair to say understanding the (mathematical) variation in data is the reason statistics exists as a field. And it's key to understanding how science is not as objective and uncreative as often depicted—and why scientific thinking can be so interesting!

NGSS Connection:
SEP4 Analyzing and interpreting data

The authors of the *Science Framework* and NGSS recognize the place of messy data, too. They highlight *analyzing and interpreting data* (SEP4) as one of the eight science and engineering practices. I've been highlighting the importance of data, messy or otherwise, throughout this book. Not surprisingly, scientists work with different kinds of data. Sometimes we describe observations through words or pictures, sometimes through numbers. In this chapter, I focus on numerical data. Even within this specification, it's useful to think about different kinds of data, each limited in the kinds of answers they can provide, what you can do with them, and how they're typically displayed.

And, if that's not enough, all this is almost certainly part of your state's math standards, too.

To illustrate types of data and their values and limitations for predicting and explaining, I turn to another classic elementary school investigation activity—observing seed germination.

Seed Germination (Exploration)

- **Overview:** Students observe seed sprouting and germination.
- **Grades:** Third and higher
- **Time needed:** Seeds will sprout over the course of several days, but actual classroom time may be limited to ~30 minutes for initial setup, a few minutes for daily observations, and time for later classroom discussion(s).

MATERIALS

- Seeds, easily available in home stores, garden centers, and some supermarkets; enough for each student to have two to four seeds
- Clear zip-style sandwich bags, at least one for each student
- Paper towels
- Water
- Paper plates (optional)

INSTRUCTIONS

Each student should

1. Moisten a paper towel, enough that it's thoroughly wet but not dripping.

2. Place 2–4 seeds on the bottom half of the towel.

3. Fold the top half of the towel over the bottom half.

4. Gently place the folded towel in the zip-style sandwich bag, and seal the bag.

5. Gently place the bag someplace in the classroom where it won't be disturbed, yet still provide students with easy access to check their seeds' sprouting. A sunny, warm window sill is a good choice. Some teachers additionally ask students to place their bags on top of paper plates.

6. At least once per day, over the next several days, gently open the bag, observe the seeds, noting which seeds have sprouted, and put everything back where it was.

What's Happening? Most seeds will absorb moisture and eventually sprout.

NGSS Connections: Performance expectations 3-LS1-1 says students who develop an understanding can develop models to describe that organisms have unique and diverse life cycles, but all have in common birth, growth, reproduction, and death.

Performance expectation 4-LS1-1 says students can construct an argument that plants and animals have internal and external structures that function to support survival, growth, behavior, and reproduction.

TRY IT!

Separate from other considerations, this investigation activity illustrates a key point about planning investigations and all that follows: to apply science and engineering practices to figure out answers to empirical questions requires *knowing* something about the topic being investigated. There's no such thing as a content-free lesson.

An important purpose of this lesson is for students to begin understanding the pros and cons of different data types, illustrated via investigations with germinating seeds. To accomplish that goal, however, requires they know something *about* germinating seeds. That's where Activity 8 comes in. By the time the investigation activity is finished, students will have experienced and observed firsthand the process of seed germination, they'll know how to set up conditions where seeds will germinate, and have begun thinking about what they need to do to make it happen again. They will have had relevant, concrete background experiences involving the topic at hand. The investigation activity thus acts as an *exploratory* activity within the 5E or learning-cycle model of instruction.

TEACHING TIPS

For this first investigation activity about seed germination, I recommend choosing something like a bean or pea seed—something moderately large, common, and familiar. Smaller seeds like radishes or mustards might be a little more difficult to work with at first, just because of their size, and we want this initial experience with the seeds to be one in which students feel successful. Ideally, their seeds will sprout and they will find the experience exciting.

To prepare for the activity, take a few seeds home and try it out yourself. You might even experiment a little on your own with paper towel dampness. If the towel isn't damp enough, seed germination may be inhibited. On the other hand, towels can be too damp, which can encourage mold growth. A little mold is not dangerous, but it's still something you might want to try minimizing.

Step 5: The seeds should be OK anyplace you'd feel physically comfortable. Very cold or hot places might be less desirable. A sunny windowsill usually works fine, although light is not strictly speaking a requirement for seed germination. (Students often believe light is necessary for all plant growth but, if you think about it, seeds are typically underground when they germinate. Living things have different requirements at different stages in their life cycles. Of course, asking "will plant seeds germinate in the dark" is an operational question children could investigate!)

Step 6: This activity is mostly about students simply observing seed germination, seeing what it looks like, and doing things like practicing gently opening their towels, observing, and putting everything back like it was. They (and you) can begin thinking about factors that might affect how long it takes seeds to germinate, things everyone will need to make sure they do the same way when the class continues their experimentation in more studies with seeds.

I suggest students record how many days it took each seed to germinate. Pool class data from all the seeds, and make a simple bar chart or dot plot as a way to represent the class dataset. The graph's *x*-axis would be the number of days it took for a seed to germinate. If a seed germinated after 2 days, place a dot or other mark in the "2" column. You could let students make marks on the class graph when they've observed their seeds sprouting. Using a picture or drawing of a seed, rather than an "X" might be a way to make the graph slightly more experience near.

Presumably, seeds will not all germinate at exactly the same time. The pooled class data will exhibit some variation, and trying to figure out an answer to the question "how long did it take our seeds to sprout" will illustrate some of the data "messiness" I mentioned earlier. Depending on your state's grade-level mathematics standards, students are expected to understand, at various levels of depth, some of the ways we try to summarize and make sense of data as well as understand the kind of variability being demonstrated here, that is, concepts like the mean, median, and range. If you're an elementary teacher, consider using this activity an opportunity to combine science and math lessons. If you're a middle school science teacher, consider coordinating this activity with your math teacher colleagues.

WHAT'S GOING ON IN THE SCIENCE?

Seeds typically absorb water, swell a little, their seed coatings break open, and the plant starts growing. They need water, air (oxygen), and a minimal amount of warmth to start the process. Although some seeds don't germinate until they have been exposed to other environmental conditions, like being charred in a forest fire or bathed in the acid of an animal's digestive system, the kinds of seeds commonly available in home stores usually do not require such extreme conditions to germinate.

At first the plant's food comes from the seed itself. Most of the seed fulfills this function; the actual embryo is fairly small. Once they're sprouted, continued growth eventually requires other factors, like light and carbon dioxide. If students are gentle, they can plant their sprouted seeds in dirt and continue observing their growth—which is kind of cool, especially if students have never seen something like this before.

To make this chapter's investigation activities align more closely with a 5E or learning-cycle model of instruction, the end of Activity 8 would be the place for the teacher to introduce these points to students, perhaps accompanied by names for the parts of the seeds they've been observing and discussing what you want them to know. This would represent the explanation or content introduction phase of the models. This might also be an appropriate place to begin discussing the concept of a plant's life cycle, from seed to plant and back again. (The Internet is full of images of germinating seeds and plant life cycles; search for "seed germination.")

CONNECTIONS TO THE NATURE OF SCIENCE

When we talk about "messiness" in data, we're really talking about data variability and the need to understand, explain, and ultimately figure out an underlying meaning for observations that are not clear cut. Franklin et al. (2007) lay out key sources for this data variability. You are probably familiar with the kind of variability that comes from sampling populations, like you find in polls, but I'm going to focus here on other sources of variability. They include

- variability that comes from repeating the same measurement on the same individual. Two children, for example, could measure the same bean seed and get different results because they used different measuring tools or measured the beans slightly different ways.

- variability that's part of nature. Three different bean seeds could all have slightly different lengths, for example. In this investigation activity, children are also observing natural variability in the time it takes for seeds to germinate—assuming all the seeds are exposed to the same conditions.

- variability that we purposefully induce. If we plant and grow beans with different amounts of water, then differences in their growth would hopefully be due to differences in how much water they received. But, theoretically, all or some of the differences could be due to natural variability from plant to plant. Or they could be due to something else, maybe something we haven't even thought about.

So, when analyzing the results from experimental investigations, scientists are essentially trying to figure out how much of the variability they observe was purposefully induced, that is, due to their experimental procedures, and how much was due to natural variation. They must further try to figure out how much of the differences observed were from the factor they were manipulating or trying to learn about (the independent variable), and how much were from other factors—uncontrolled variables or

> **Key Takeaway**
>
> Experimental data interpretation involves figuring out how much of observed differences were from the experiment and how much were not.

unknown factors that might affect their results. Often scientists need to repeat their investigations, perform them differently, or think about their results differently to deal with this issue. Science is frequently far from the straightforward, cut and dried process it's made out to be. That's part of what makes it so interesting.

Key Takeaway

Data variation is natural and expected.

I leave to your discretion how deeply you wish to discuss with your class the concept of variation among results. All students, however—even lower elementary students—should learn that results vary and this natural variation is expected—it's part of science and natural phenomena.

Older students can also learn that the kinds of conclusions discussed in school science and textbooks are so widely accepted that we present them as if certain. We say "The Earth moves around the Sun" and "Genes encode blueprints for proteins." Textbooks discuss ideas that have been confirmed over and over, sometimes for hundreds of years. All scientific knowledge must be considered tentative, it might change someday, but the scientific ideas generally presented in school seem pretty unlikely to change anytime in the near future.

For scientists doing science, however, the story is a bit different. Trying to learn something new, their conclusions are often a lot more tentative. The data supporting them is much less clear cut. Sometimes it can be downright

Key Takeaway

Scientists express findings honestly with language representing the strength of the data supporting their conclusions.

murky. Being honest people, they have to present their findings with language accurately representing the strength of the data supporting their conclusions. So scientists speak in terms of probabilities, they use what Bowen and Bartley (2014) call "hedging language." I'll show you what I mean in the sections that follow.

PRACTICES IN PRACTICE

By now you undoubtedly recognize any good investigation activity requires that students apply multiple science and engineering practices. Perhaps you can even identify SEPs students are using in this activity. Rather than listing them this time, I'll just focus on one SEP.

NGSS Connection:
SEP8 Obtaining, evaluating, and communicating information

Once scientists start figuring out what to make of their data, they need to tell others about it to find out whether they interpret the data similarly. *Obtaining, evaluating, and communicating information* is the eighth SEP. I mentioned the idea of displaying class data with a bar chart or dot plot. Graphs,

LEARNING SCIENCE BY DOING SCIENCE

charts, tables, and other visual devices are important ways scientists—and everyone else—communicate arguments and the evidence supporting them. We *all* need to be graphically literate!

NGSS's Appendix F discusses differences in expectations for students' abilities to analyze and display data across grade levels.

- **In the 3–5 classroom:** Students in Grades 3–5 represent data in tables and bar graphs.
- **In the 6–8 classroom:** Students progress to examining larger or more complex datasets, which include beginning to distinguish between causal and correlational relationships in data. This latter point—so vital for anyone who ever examines any kind of empirical data—means students will also be representing data via scatterplots, the kinds of graphs with horizontal and vertical axes combined with dots representing data.

In the next part of the chapter I'm drawing on Michael Bowen and Anthony Bartley's (2014) *The Basics of Data Literacy.* The authors point out that part of the difficulty students have in understanding graphical data stems from data's abstractness; many graphs are removed from students' everyday experiences—they are "experience distant." The next investigation activities—designed to help you and your students understand different types of data—might also help make the data and its representation a little more "experience near."

Seed Germination, Categorical Variable (Expansion)

Overview: Students compare germination times for two to three different kinds of plant seeds.

Grades: Third and higher

Time needed: Seeds will sprout over the course of several days, but actual classroom time may be limited to 30 minutes for initial setup, a few minutes for daily observations, and time for later classroom discussion(s).

MATERIALS

- Two to three different kinds of plant seeds, easily available in home stores, garden centers, and some supermarkets; enough for each student to have at least one of each plant seed
- Clear zip-style sandwich bags, at least one for each student
- Paper towels
- Water
- Paper plates (optional)

INSTRUCTIONS

1. Students should follow basically the same directions as in the first activity in this chapter, except each student should germinate two or three different kinds of plant seeds so they can observe any differences in germination times between the two species of plants.

2. Younger children can observe whether or not each of their seeds germinated after 2 or perhaps 3 days; you can pool class data for the overall comparison and make a bar graph showing how many of each seed type germinated. Older children might observe how many days it took each of their seeds to germinate, again pooling class data for the overall comparison and making a dot plot.

What's Happening? Natural variation exists in germination times for different plant species.

NGSS Connections: Performance expectation 3-LS1-1 says students who demonstrate an understanding develop models to describe that organisms have unique and diverse life cycles, but all have in common birth, growth, reproduction, and death.

Performance expectation 4-LS1-1 says students construct an argument that plants and animals have internal and external structures that function to support survival, growth, behavior, and reproduction.

Categorical, or nominal, variables are variables with two or more categories, and no inherent order to the categories.

Scientists and mathematicians use the words *nominal* or *categorical* to represent variables that are in separate categories without any particular order. For example, if you measured the absorbency of four brands of paper towels, or compared the growth of plants in light and dark conditions, you would be changing categorical variables. There's no obvious order to those paper towels or plants.

In this case of Activity 8.1, the two or three different kinds of seeds serve as a categorical variable. Investigations with categorical variables are quite useful. Studies often group test subjects into two or more separate and independent groups for comparison. A study comparing two classrooms, or men and women, or plants grown under different conditions are all comparing a categorical variable.

Nevertheless, categorical variables are still limited in some ways. If students compared, say, germination time for corn and radish seeds, there's no inherent order for the seed types and you can't find an average for "corn" and "radish." You *could* use the data to make predictions about how long it would take other corn or radish seeds to sprout, but the data wouldn't allow you to make any kind of educated guess about sprouting time for any *other* kind of plant. You can't extrapolate data from one kind of seed to another.

Displaying the class's data in a table or bar graph is the kind of representation that NGSS's authors discuss as appropriate for younger children to work with. So, if you are teaching in a self-contained classroom or work closely with a math teacher, this could be an appropriate time for a lesson about bar graphs. Some young children often work with dot plots as well, so you can consider that variation.

Class data about germination times for two or three different kinds of seeds would be a dataset with multiple categories. Because K–8 teachers report feeling more comfortable with math than science, and are more likely to have participated in math than science professional development recently, I leave to you discussion about strategies to introduce students to different kinds of graphical displays. However, in Figure 7.1, I provide example graphical displays showing results of a hypothetical Activity 8.1. In this example, students have kept track of how many days it took each seed to germinate, class data were pooled, and ultimately data about 14 A seeds and 12 B seeds were available.

I created two graphs. One of the graphs is a traditional bar graph, showing the median, or middle, number of days it took each sample of seeds to germinate. I chose the median because it's a little less abstract than the mean. The B seeds seem to have germinated faster than the A seeds.

However, I also included dots to represent how many days each of the 14 A and 12 B seeds took to germinate. It still seems very probably that B's germinate faster than A's, but the conclusion is a little less clear cut when all the data points are on display. This kind of variation is what I've been discussing. Reallife conclusions don't always jump out as obvious when examining a graph or table.

If scientists were discussing these data, they might not say "B's germinate faster than A's." They might, instead, use hedging language and say something like "it's probable that B's germinate faster than A's," or "data currently support the conclusion B's germinate faster than A's."

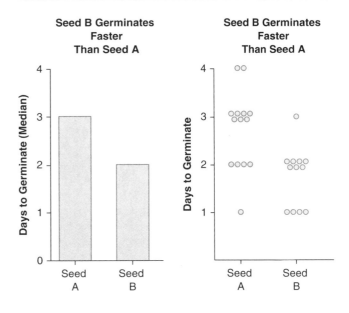

FIGURE 7.1 Categorical Data

Seed Germination, Ordered Variable (Expansion)

Overview: Students compare germination times for three to four different-sized plant seeds.

Grades: Third and higher

Time needed: Seeds will sprout over the course of several days, but actual classroom time may be limited to ~30 minutes for initial setup, a few minutes for daily observations, and time for later classroom discussion(s).

MATERIALS

- At least three different kinds of plant seeds—small, medium, and larger sized—easily available in home stores, garden centers, and some supermarkets; enough for each student to have at least one of each plant seed.
- Clear zip-style sandwich bags, at least one for each student
- Paper towels
- Water
- Paper plates (optional)

INSTRUCTIONS

1. Give students at least three different kinds of plant seeds, chosen on the basis of their sizes. Radish and mustard seeds are small, so are some types of tomatoes. Corn, peas, pumpkin, and watermelon are medium. Beans are often large. Have students arrange their seeds from smallest to largest. Because some seeds are flat but wide, some judgment may be involved.

2. Students should follow basically the same directions as in the first activity in this chapter, except each student should germinate two or three different kinds of plant seeds so they can observe any differences in germination times between the two species of plants.

3. Younger children can observe whether or not each of their seeds germinated after 2 or perhaps 3 days; you can pool class data for the overall comparison. Older children can observe how many days it

took each of their seeds to germinate, again pooling class data for the overall comparison.

What's Happening? Natural variation exists in germination times for different plant species. Smaller seeds often germinate faster than larger seeds. Small seeds have less stored food than large seeds. Plant survival depends on having roots and leaves before their stored food is gone.

NGSS Connections: Performance expectation 3-LS1-1 says students who demonstrate an understanding develop models to describe that organisms have unique and diverse life cycles but all have in common birth, growth, reproduction, and death.

Performance expectation 4-LS1-1 says students construct an argument that plants and animals have internal and external structures that function to support survival, growth, behavior, and reproduction.

ORDERED VARIABLES

Ordered or ordinal variables are variables with separate categories, but an inherent order to the categories.

Scientists and mathematicians use the terms *ordered* or *ordinal* to describe variables that are still in separate categories, but categories with some inherent order to them. In the case of Activity 8.2, ordering seeds as small, medium, and large serves as an ordered variable. Grouping people on the basis of income categories (lower class, middle class, upper class) would also be an example of an ordered variable, as are comparisons of race results (A was first, B was second, etc.).

Likert-style survey questions are also common sources of ordered variables. For example, consider this question:

To what extent are you likely to try inquiry-based instruction as a result of reading this book?

(a) I will not try inquiry.

(b) I might try inquiry.

(c) I will probably try inquiry.

(d) I will definitely try inquiry.

FIGURE 7.2 Ordered Data

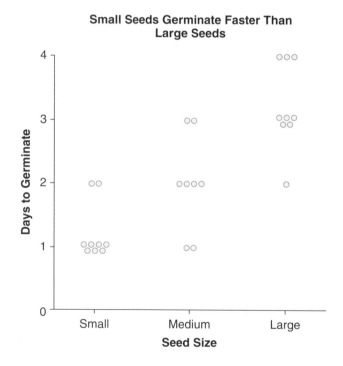

Responses fall into four categories (a, b, c, and d), and there's an inherent order to the responses. But the responses aren't numbers, they don't act like numbers. You can't really say, for example, response (c) is somehow three times larger than response (a). Similarly, going from responses (a) to (b) does not necessarily represent the same difference as going from responses (b) to (c). For this kind of data, statisticians often point out, a simple mean or average does not necessarily provide an accurate summary.

Figure 7.2 shows a graph showing (hypothetical) results for an investigation germinating small, medium, and large seeds.

If you were working with younger children or children you felt not yet developmentally ready to understand this kind of graph, you could again count how many small, medium, and large seeds had germinated after a given amount of time, plot the data on a bar graph (or dot plot), and work with that instead.

Ordered variables are more useful than categorical variables for forming conclusions and making predictions. My hypothetical data, for example, shows a trend indicating seed size might very well be linked to germination time. (See how I used hedging language a little?) I could not, however, make detailed predictions about germination time for other types of seeds. If small seeds germinated in about a day, and medium seeds germinated in 2 days, more or less, you might predict seeds whose size was somewhere between small and medium would germinate in more than 1, but still less than 2 days on average. Any finer grade distinction, however, would not be supported by the available data.

For these finer grade distinctions, you need numeric data.

Seed Germination, Numeric Variable (Expansion)

Overview: Students compare germination times of the same kind of seed.

Grades: Third and higher

Time needed: Seeds will sprout over the course of several days, but actual classroom time may be limited to ~30 minutes for initial setup, a few minutes for daily observations, and time for later classroom discussion(s).

MATERIALS

- Plant seeds, easily available in home stores, garden centers, and some supermarkets; enough for each student to have five to ten of the same kind of seed
- Clear zip-style sandwich bags, at least one for each student
- Paper towels
- Water
- Bowls
- Paper plates (optional)
- Permanent markers (optional)

INSTRUCTIONS

1. At the beginning of the school day, place at least one seed for every student in a bowl of room temperature water. Repeat the process, placing seeds in different bowls, approximately 1, 2, 3, and 4 hours later. After 5 hours, you'll have five bowls, one with seeds that soaked 1 hour, one with seeds that soaked 2 hours, etc.

2. Five hours after initially placing seeds in water, give students one seed from each bowl. In other words, one seed that has presoaked for 5 hours, one that's presoaked for four hours, etc.

3. (Optional) Also give students a seed that has not been presoaked at all, to act as a control for comparison.

4. Students should take their seeds and follow basically the same directions as in the first activity in this chapter, except the seeds need to be marked on their paper towels so students will know how long each

seed presoaked. One option is to mark the paper towels at the places particular seeds are to be placed (seed soaked for 1 hour, seed soaked for 2 hours, etc.). Students should be slightly more careful handling their damp towels to decrease the chance seeds will move around.

5. Younger children can observe whether or not each of their seeds germinated after 2 or perhaps 3 days; you can pool class data for the overall comparison. Older children can observe how many days it took each of their seeds to germinate, again pooling class data for the overall comparison.

What's Happening? Students are investigating whether and how presoaking times affect germination speed. Some seeds germinate faster after longer presoaking.

NGSS Connections: 3-LS1-1. Develop models to describe that organisms have unique and diverse life cycles but all have in common birth, growth, reproduction, and death.

4-LS1-1. Construct an argument that plants and animals have internal and external structures that function to support survival, growth, behavior, and reproduction.

NUMERIC VARIABLES

Numeric variables are number measurements.

Scientists and mathematics refer to the kind of variable students are manipulating or changing in this investigation activity as a **numerical** (sometimes the terms **continuous** or **ratio-level** are also used to describe this type of variable). Basically, it's numbers. A measurement of 4 is twice as large as a measurement of 2, the difference between a 2 and a 3 is the same as the difference between a 3 and a 4, etc. In our example, students are comparing seeds that have presoaked for 0, 1, 2, 3, 4, and 5 hours.

In my graph of hypothetical data, the data indicate a trend toward faster germination when seeds have been presoaked.

Numerical variables are even more useful than ordered variables for forming conclusions and making predictions. Unlike categorical or ordered variables, numerical variables permit more detailed or exacting predictions. The data would allow you to predict how seeds might behave after, say, 1½ hours of presoaking. Or if you knew how long a seed had presoaked, you might be able to tentatively predict how long it would take until it germinated.

As powerful as that is, there's still a subjective, interpretive aspect even with data like this. In Figure 7.3 you'll see two lines showing apparent trends in the data; one line is solid and the other is dotted. Do you think one better represents the apparent relationship between presoaking time (the independent variable) and germination time (dependent variable)? If these data were being presented by scientists at, say, a conference, the researchers would present their data, present their interpretation of their data (via a graph, complete with whatever line they believe best shows apparent trends in their data), explain why they believed as they did, and then let the rest of the scientific community decide whether they accept the interpretation. All the data should be available for everyone to interpret as they see fit; the process is transparent. *That's* how science works.

FIGURE 7.3 Numerical Data

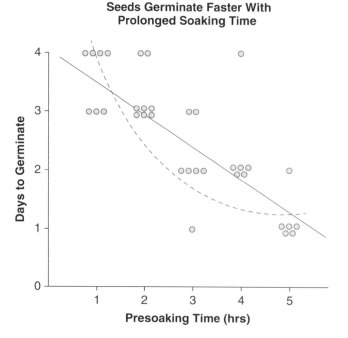

Seeds Germinate Faster With Prolonged Soaking Time

CONCLUSION

As students complete investigations, they will generate data. Even the youngest students will ultimately be examining their data and looking for patterns, they will be trying to make meaning from it. Scientists (and nonscientists!) often use graphs and tables to help them figure out their data's meaning—and communicate their findings to everyone else. They also use their graphical displays to predict what will happen as a result in other investigations, one of the hallmarks of science. Investigations changing categorical and ordered variables are quite valuable, but usually less powerful for making predictions than those changing numeric variables. Younger children can usually understand categorical and ordered data, and the resulting bar graphs or dot plots, more readily than numeric data, and the resulting scatterplot-type graphs.

In judging the developmental appropriateness of an investigation, pay attention to the kind of data students will create, as well as how removed the investigation and its data are from students' everyday lives. The further the investigation and data are from students' lives, the less likely they will be to understand—and *any* graph abstracts experience.

Recognize, further, that real-life investigations usually do not produce the kinds of neat data found in contrived school cookbook-type lab activities. And that's OK. Embrace the messiness! It makes interpreting data a little more subjective, more in need of discussion and argument with evidence, more in need of analysis and creativity—a little more in need of the human touch.

Additional Resources

Although simply searching the Web for "seed germination experiment paper towels" or "seed germination plastic bag" will yield many resources, http://my.chicagobotanic.org/education/youth_ed/eleven-experiments-with-radish-seeds/ provides several example questions that students could investigate.

Chapter 8

Bob the Builder and You

What about engineering and NGSS?

In this section, you will come to see how

- engineering is about applying scientific ideas to real-world problems.

You will be able to

- help your students recognize that scientific ideas can be applied to the world outside their classroom.

Engineering and technology is one of the NGSS aspects teachers find most foreign and frightening. I know I certainly did. I found myself thinking, "I'm a science teacher, not an engineer!" You may be thinking, "I don't even understand science, how am I going to teach engineering too?!" But it doesn't have to be frightening. In fact, with a better understanding of the NGSS goals for the topic, it's possible you might even decide it's your favorite part of the entire document!

The authors of the framework underlying NGSS stress that a science education focusing only on science facts—the products of science—is incomplete. It needs to also focus on *where* those facts came from and *what* we can do with them. Most of this book has focused on the former; I've spent little time discussing the latter point. This is where NGSS's conception of engineering and technology comes in.

The *Science Framework* does not discuss engineering as something separate from science. In fact, the core idea in the document related to engineering is named "Engineering, Technology and Application of Science." The *Framework's* authors are writing about using scientific knowledge. They're addressing two age old questions students and teachers have pondered for years:

- Why do I need to know this stuff?
- When am I ever going to use this?

For the first question, the *Science Framework's* Chapter 8 mentions all sorts of practical applications where people use scientific knowledge and abilities, including:

- designing a product,
- designing an (industrial or commercial) process,
- designing a medical treatment,
- designing new technology,
- evaluating or predicting the impact of something we're doing, or
- even doing more science.

Science impacts technology and society in myriad ways, and often, engineering is the link between scientific knowledge and its practical applications in our everyday lives. This is one of the core ideas in the *Science Framework* related to engineering.

Key Takeaway

Engineering is the link between scientific knowledge and its practical application.

With the *Framework* as the source document in the creation of NGSS, NGSS's authors ultimately folded the idea into other disciplinary core ideas and performance expectations, rather than keeping it separate. NGSS's middle school storyline for the Engineering, Technology and Applications of Science core idea says

> [I]n the life sciences students apply their engineering design capabilities to evaluate plans for maintaining biodiversity and ecosystem services. . . . In the physical sciences students define and solve problems involving a number of core ideas in physical science, including: chemical processes that release or absorb energy . . . Newton's third law of motion . . . and energy transfer. . . . In the Earth and space sciences students apply their engineering design capabilities to problems related the impacts of humans on Earth systems. (NGSS Lead States, 2013c)

The primary idea relates to the "when am I ever going to use this stuff" question. Engineering design is about solving problems—the kind of real-life problems where one needs to understand some science. Designing and making solutions to lots of real-life problems requires using scientific knowledge and practices.

So how does this play out in the classroom? If you've read other chapters in this book, you've already learned about one engineering activity: the investigation activity where students learn about electrical circuits (Chapter 2). The activity begins with students trying to design a solution to solve a problem: making a light bulb light, and then it continues as they design ever more increasingly complex circuits lighting two bulbs, perhaps more, perhaps adding switches to control the lights.

Now let's explore a different—but equally fun, equally useful—engineering problem where students explore design principles holding up everyday structures like homes, bridges, towers, tents, and even cardboard boxes!

Structures

Overview: Students build increasingly large cubes from straws and paper clips, learning about tension, compression, and shapes associated with rigid structures.

Grades: Second and higher

Time needed: 30–90 minutes, depending on extension investigation activities in Step 5.

MATERIALS

- Straws (straight, not the flexible kind)
- Paper clips
- Styrofoam or paper cups, and pennies or other small weights to put in the cups and hang from parts of structures for testing purposes (optional)
- Straight pins (optional)

INSTRUCTIONS

1. Have students make a square that's one straw wide. Use paper clips to join straws together. (Push the side of a clip into the end of a straw, slide a second clip onto the first one, and slide the second straw onto the end of the second clip.)

FIGURE 8.1 Structures 1

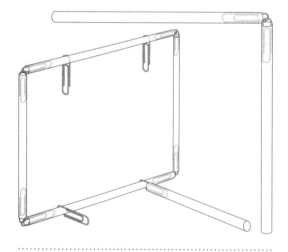

Paper clips and straws joined for making structures

2. The resulting square will lack the rigidity it needs to hold its shape and ultimately act as a wall holding up a "building." Students experiment with adding additional straws to their squares, investigating what patterns of added straws do to keep the square rigid and "unbendy."

3. Students go on to apply what they learned about braces (diagonal straws that create triangles) by building a cube one straw long, wide, and high. The cube should be able to stand on its own. I usually allow students as many straws as they like, with straws beyond the 12 needed to make a cube

held in place the same way they were in the previous part of the activity, via paper clips or pins.

4. After successfully making a 1 × 1 × 1 straw structure, students apply what they have learned to create a larger structure, a 3 × 3 × 3 straw cube.

5. After students have made 3 × 3 × 3 structures, and you've had a classroom discussion about how making a 3 × 3 × 3 structure differed from a 1 × 1 × 1 structure, and then compared student designs—their literal strengths and weaknesses—the activity can continue many different ways. Your schedule, interests, student goals, and assessment of students' interests can help you decide between

- Students trying to improve their designs, seeing if they can build stronger structures

- Students trying to improve their designs, seeing if they can build equally strong structures using fewer straws

- Students trying to add roofs onto a 3 × 3 × 3 structures, testing what effects (if any) various designs have on the strength or stability of structures

- Students can hang weights off different parts of their structures to more systematically and quantitatively investigate the strength of their structures, finding places the structures are stronger (more rigid) and weaker (less rigid, or more likely to fall apart).

- Students can try to alter their designs to withstand shaking, simulating an earthquake.

What's Happening? The key to solid structures in this activity lies in corners being held rigidly in place. Diagonal straws, forming triangles, are important for creating the necessary rigidity.

NGSS Connections: Although this investigation activity approaches performance expectation 3-PS2-1, which says students who demonstrate an understanding can plan and conduct an investigation to provide evidence of the effects of balanced and unbalanced forces on the motion of an object, it most closely aligns with the *Framework's* PS2.A Forces and Motion and PS2.C Motion and Stability disciplinary core ideas.

TRY IT!

Children have been designing and testing towers, bridges, houses, and similar structures for generations. "Structures" was a unit in the Elementary Science Study in the 1960s, with children building structures out of clay, straws, pins, paper tubes, and index cards (Elementary Science Study, 1970). They never stopped building, with books and curricula appearing each decade that followed.

This investigation activity, as described, aligns somewhat with the 5E or learning-cycle model of instruction. Steps 1–4 are *exploratory*, with students testing their thinking about what helps hold up structures like buildings, applying their learning in increasingly complex structures. To make the classroom activity align more strongly with the 5E or learning-cycle model, the teacher would probably accent pushing and pulling forces as part of the discussion at the beginning of Step 5, and then try to explicitly have students use that knowledge (and the new terminology) in completing the rest of the step.

TEACHING TIPS

Step 1: Straws are inexpensive, easily found, large enough to be fun, and small enough to not take over a classroom. I favor joining them with paper clips rather than materials like pins, clay, or candy gumdrops. Paper clips may be safer than pins, and dealing with the floppiness they offer when joining straws together presents a challenge illustrating important principles of architectural design and building stability.

Step 2: When students add additional straws to make their "walls" rigid, they can attach the additional straws using paper clips (as illustrated), or straight pins. If you believe your students can safely handle pins, they are slightly more convenient to work with for this part of the activity. As with every investigation activity in this book, try it out ahead of time yourself before deciding.

Students can begin testing and understanding what's going on regarding parts of their walls being pushed, pulled, or otherwise held rigidly in place by simply pressing on the straws. By pressing on various parts of their "walls," students get data about the effects of their investigations. Added straws might make structures more rigid at corners (where straws are linked together by paper clips) or in the middle of their "walls," in between corners. The added rigidity might be found everywhere, or just certain parts of the "walls."

You might want to add a classroom discussion to gather together and discuss what students tried for making their "walls" more rigid, what happened as a result, and help them recognize patterns and tentative generalizations. Generally speaking, diagonally placed straws—forming triangles—add more strength to structures than straws placed vertically or horizontally, all else being equal. (Diagonal elements, whose purposes are to support or hold other parts of a framework in position, are often called "braces.")

FIGURE 8.2 Structures 2

Step 3: After students successfully make their structures, you may have individual or whole-class discussions about what students did, what they were thinking along the way, and what they are thinking about their designs now that they have finished. You may also decide to have individual or whole-group discussions comparing different designs, helping students (and yourself!) understand how different design elements affect the shape, rigidity, and stability of the resulting structure.

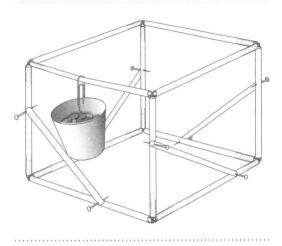

Structure supporting a load

You can, optionally, have (some?) students test the strengths of their designs more quantitatively by hanging a Styrofoam cup (held in place by a bent paper clip) from various part of their structures. Nails, pennies, or other small weights can be added to the cup; stronger modifications will produce cups holding more weight before straws start to bend.

You can help more advanced students understand there's subjectivity in merely saying something like "when we added 16 pennies to the cup, the top straw bent." To fairly compare the effects of adding, say, a vertically placed extra straw versus a diagonally placed one, students would want to observe carefully how much straws bent. Alternatively, pennies could be added to a cup one by one until a straw has bent a given amount, comparing how much weight it takes in each test until the straws looked like they bent more or less the same.

At this and later steps in the investigation activity, students finishing early can be challenged to make their structure just as strong, or even stronger, while using *fewer* straws.

Step 4: Once again, the resulting structure should be strong and stable enough to stand on its own, and students will use additional straws to make the structure freestanding. You may, optionally, require students to sketch out their designs before beginning, perhaps also jotting down (or telling you about) thoughts regarding why they are adding additional straws, predicting the effects the straws will have on the structure. This provides you with some insight into their thinking, while forcing students to invest and commit to a design.

Building a 3 × 3 × 3 straw cube is a nice activity for encouraging students to work together. It's virtually impossible for an individual to make the structure.

It needs more than one pair of hands. That said, some groups may struggle a little with keeping their structure from collapsing. That's OK, but if students are struggling enough that they are becoming frustrated, you can help them by having them back up and consider one wall or side of their model. Ask students about where they could add straws to keep the side rigid, to keep it from wobbling. You can encourage them to use what they learned when working on a 1 × 1 × 1 structure, or look at what other groups are doing. This is not a competition; it's OK to observe others' efforts and learn from them. If necessary, you can show students how diagonals add rigidity to their structures.

As students are working, you can also ask them about which parts of their structures bend most easily and least easily when pressed upon. Pressing or pushing on parts of the structure is also called applying a force. Real-life structures must constantly withstand forces, referred to as supporting a load. So, when students press on parts of their structures to see how rigid they feel, or hang weights off parts of their structures to examine how much mass they can hold without bending much, they are testing the structure's capacity to support various loads.

Step 5: As before, teachers sometimes require students draw (and explain) a design before building structures. Alternatively, students might be required to draw designs *after* successfully building their structures. If students investigated their structures' strengths, you might ask them to make this information part of their diagrams.

Teachers also sometimes turn (part of) this activity into a contest, seeing who can design and build a strong and stable structure with the fewest number of straws. One definition of a stable structure might be the ability to pick it up and rotate it 90 degrees. This mimics engineering challenges, where material limitations may affect what's possible. A similar variation would be seeing who can make a structure using the fewest pins (or paper clips, if you're not using pins). Since each pin represents a place someone had to attach an additional straw, this mimics limitations on the labor costs in creating a structure.

Creative teachers might even find ways to combine these factors, challenging students to make a strong, stable 3 × 3 × 3 cube structure with the fewest number of straws *and* pins, perhaps counting the costs of straws and pins differently, essentially weighting how much they count toward the total used to complete the project.

A similar option, simulating real life, is to provide students with a price list for straws, paper clips, pins, and any other materials they will need, and a budget for the total amount they may spend to build their structure. To encourage inquiry-based investigation, you might put the budgetary constraints only on the final product. Students can experiment with whatever materials they like; they are only limited when presenting their final designs.

Finally, extension activities where students apply some of the same design principles they learned building cube shaped structures include lessons where students build bridges or towers, or investigate building structures that can withstand shaking (earthquakes) or high winds (simulated by a fan).

WHAT'S GOING ON IN THE SCIENCE?

This activity, of course, illustrates engineering design principles. It does, however, also connect to disciplinary core ideas, probably most strongly to the *Science Framework's* core ideas PS2.A, which is about forces and motion, and PS2.C, about stability and instability in physical systems. As described in the *Framework*, objects that are connected push and pull on each other. In this case, scientists would say gravity pushes down on the straws (and paper clips), and the table top pushes back anywhere the straws are pushing down. With these forces as starting points, the straws (and paper clips) push and pull on each other. Since the structure is just sitting there, it's a static object. The various forces acting on it add up to zero. Except when they don't—in which case it'll move, probably collapsing, until the forces once again add up to zero.

Adding a load to the structure adds new forces. And, of course, gravity pushes down on the structure, while the table or floor underneath the straws pushes up.

By the end of second grade, the *Science Framework* suggests that students should understand objects push or pull on one another when they are connected, and that the pushes and pulls can have different strengths and directions. By the end of fifth grade, students should also recognize how an object, like the straw structure, can have multiple forces acting on it—multiple pushes and pulls—that add to give a net force of zero. The forces balance each other. If they didn't add to zero, the object would be changing its speed or direction, collapsing or at least shifting positions.

I interpret this to mean that if students are designing and investigating straw structures, and you are helping them explore forces acting on the straws, then the activities will be in line with NGSS expectations. Generally speaking, the forces probably fall mostly into two broad categories—places where straws are being compressed (i.e., pushed or squished together) and stretched (or pulled apart).

CONNECTIONS TO THE NATURE OF SCIENCE (AND ENGINEERING!)

It's true that engineering design isn't exactly the same as doing science. Engineers start with tasks, problems to solve—things to design, build, and test—and end with solutions. Scientists, on the other hand, start with questions to answer—puzzling phenomena to explore or explanations to test—and end with answers.

Science is about exploring, explaining, and understanding phenomena; engineering is about applying. As different as that may sound, they've got an awful lot in common. Both processes are ultimately empirical and hands-on. To know if an engineering problem has been solved, you have to test it. Both require creativity, planning, testing, analyzing, and more testing. Both require being open to change. Both use models. Both are social, involve communicating and arguing from evidence.

Engineering design starts with a problem, a clear problem with specific criteria—so classroom engineering should, too. This analogy may not be perfect, but the concept of beginning with clear endpoint criteria in mind will resonate with any teacher who's given an assignment having first created a rubric or other grading standard, or planned a unit by starting with outcome objectives or standards.

In the real world there are also always limitations or constraints—also equally true in classrooms. Anytime we teach a hands-on activity, we grapple with constraints—limitations on amount and kinds of materials we can provide students, safety constraints, classroom management constraints, etc.

Engineers brainstorm possible solutions, maybe making models to test out ideas before trying to actually solve the problem. Engineers and engineering design also recognize the first solution may not be the best solution. Design tweaking—or even starting over—aren't just allowed, they are required. This is what people mean when they discuss engineering as an "iterative process." Problems often have more than one solution, and figuring out what constitutes the "best" solution isn't always easy or clear cut. So we should support a similar kind of iterative process in the classroom.

NGSS Connection:
SEP1 Asking questions and defining problems

NGSS Connection:
SEP6 Constructing explanations and designing solutions

PRACTICES IN PRACTICE

Two of NGSS's eight science and engineering practices specifically mention engineering:

- SEP1: Asking questions (for science) and defining problems (for engineering)
- SEP6: Constructing explanations (for science) and designing solutions (for engineering)

The other six practices are the same. So, instead of being given a question to investigate (or coming up with their own questions to investigate), students are given a problem to solve (or come up with their own problems to solve). In this case, the problem involves designing a $1 \times 1 \times 1$ freestanding straw "house." Similarly, instead of ending with an empirically supported explanation, the engineering investigation ends with an empirically tested solution to the original problem. In this case, that means building and testing a freestanding "house."

Key Takeaway

Science starts with a question to answer; engineering starts with a problem to solve.

The *Science Framework* provides guidance about what Grade 3–5 and 6–8 students should be expected to know and understand about the engineering design process.

- **Students in Grade 5** should understand how there are constraints on solutions and that they need to meet particular criteria. They should understand the value of thinking, researching, talking together, and trying things out before designing a solution. And they should recognize you need to try out different solutions before you know which one is best.

- **Students in Grade 8** can more deeply appreciate the importance of clear and specific criteria when solving a problem. They better understand the value of testing possible solutions, recognizing that sometimes one might even take something from one solution, something else from an alternate solution, and combine them into something better than either on its own. They understand and accept just how iterative the design process can be.

Case in Point

Science and Its Applications

The *Framework* discusses using scientific knowledge, applying it toward practical ends. Engineering is defined in terms of practical uses defining and solving problems. To me it seems like examples usually relate to the physical sciences. But they don't have to do so. Scientists, including biologists, often employ engineering principles in their own work. That's why I wanted to end this chapter with an example—from the life sciences.

Earlier in the chapter, I quoted from an NGSS document noting how "in the life sciences students apply their engineering design capabilities to evaluate plans for maintaining biodiversity and ecosystem services." Although my biology colleague undoubtedly thinks of herself as neither an engineer nor as someone having any professional connections with engineering, NGSS's authors might argue otherwise.

Meet Christine Whitcraft, ecologist. Christine knew she wanted to be an ecologist by the time she was 10 years old. She loved exploring the forest near the house she grew up in, especially the crayfish in a nearby creek.

Remarkably, those feelings haven't changed. As a grown-up, tenured college professor, she still loves playing in the mud. But she also appreciates how ecology is an applied science. It's not just facts and figures to her; she believes answers to the kinds of scientific questions she investigates are directly applicable elsewhere. So I asked her about an example of what she meant.

She told me about the restoration of a local wetland she's been working on for several years. The area had been developed, but construction separating the dry land from the ocean was to be removed and the native wetlands restored. Starting before the project began, she asked the overarching question: How does a wetland recover? What path does it take, or as she and her colleagues would put it, what is the wetland "restoration trajectory"? How fast can a wetland recover to what it once was?

NGSS Connection: SEP1 Asking questions and defining problems

In many ways, however, the work also centers on a problem: How does one know when the wetland is "recovered"? It's a practical question because, once recovered, the restoration process is essentially over. The nature (and probably amounts) of public and private expenditures change.

How does one go about answering questions like these? The starting point, before the restoration began, was to ask "What's it like now?" What are the initial conditions? At some level, the answer to the question is simple: Find everything that's there and catalog it. Those are the initial conditions.

NGSS Connection: SEP3 Planning and carrying out investigations

Simple on paper, but more complex out in the field. (What's "everything"? How do you know? How do you decide?) Thus began an investigation of mud. And fish guts. And plants. And everything else that was present in this place she was studying. She was trying to do a census of every living thing she could.

She wanted to know not only what was there, but also what everybody was doing—were the plants and animals feeding? Growing? Reproducing? Her census addressed not only what she could *find*, but information about what the plants and animals were *doing* regarding the basic biological processes in which we all engage.

And then the restoration began. Construction companies came with big shovels. Backhoes. Excavators. Large earth movements destroyed a sea well; the ocean and the land were no longer separated.

A year later, she came back and did it all again. A year after that, she did it yet again. And again. Flash forward 5 years. There's been drought, there's been rain. Things are changing—some fast, some slow.

Given this, I asked her how she knows when an ecosystem is considered to have "recovered"? When will her question be answered? She told me about another restoration site that's 22 years old that they were using for comparison. She and her colleagues believe it's the best guess for what local wetlands were like in the past, so it acts as a reference point for figuring out when the work will be finished. "Sometimes," she said, "you have to go with the best site you can, even if it's not pristine."

To assess how recovered an ecosystem is, data from the site being studied are compared with data from a reference site.

NGSS Connection:
SEP4 Analyzing and interpreting data

It's like comparing data from experimental and control groups in a laboratory experiment to investigate how fast an ecosystem can recover after being extensively altered. If one wanted to set up a classical experiment to investigate the question, it would begin with two identical ecosystems. One would be destroyed, the other left alone. Over time, one would monitor what was happening in the "experimental" ecosystem that was recovering, comparing observations with those of the "control" ecosystem that had been left alone. Of course, this is not possible to do on a large scale. Christine was doing the next best thing, taking advantage of an ecosystem judged to be recovered, that is, this is the "control" ecosystem.

She can compare the growth rates of specific plants at her wetlands with those at the comparison wetlands, how many fish there are and what they're eating at both sites, how many snails there are and how fast they're reproducing, etc. Data point after data point can be compared.

NGSS Connection:
SEP6 Constructing explanations and designing solutions

Putting it all together, she creates a model to understand the wetland's restoration trajectory—a model to address her original research question. We think of school models as drawings and simple diagrams, while "real" scientific models are more abstract representations, maybe with high level math symbols thrown in sometimes. But her model looked a lot simpler than that to me. I saw a handful of photos connected by arrows. The arrows represent time, and the photos represent what's happening in the ecosystem—literal snapshots of what's alive. Comparing her model with those of other scientists studying how ecosystems recover, scientists can search for patterns and begin generalizing about the topic.

NGSS Connection:
SEP2 Developing and using models

The true health of an ecosystem, however, is ultimately more than just a row-by-row comparison of data points. With all the data that have been collected, some data must ultimately be judged more important than others. While science is so often portrayed as being very objective, there's actually often a good deal of judgment and subjectivity involved, including interpreting data—turning data into evidence supporting or refuting an argument. The health of a plant that dozens of animals depend upon for survival, for example, is deemed more important than that of a plant that nothing else depends upon. On the other hand, what does that say about the importance of the insect responsible for pollinating the plant responsible for feeding dozens of animals? This subjectivity is tempered by extensive knowledge and expertise, discussion, and peer review, but it is present in all science.

Ecologists like Christine recognize the point. It's close to the surface in her research because she knows we often view an ecosystem, like wetlands being restored, as having a "purpose." Maybe the purpose of the wetlands, for example, is to provide habitat for endangered species of local birds, which means the birds' survival, reproduction, and general health would be judged as particularly important as part of the ecosystem's restoration. We're faced with questions about how to weigh the reasons for restoring a wetland. And that, in turn, requires input from a public understanding not just ecological principles—a broad topic area addressed in *many* disciplinary core ideas—but also an understanding of what science can and cannot do to help us make decisions.

CONCLUSION

Science is about exploring, explaining, predicting, and otherwise understanding the observable world. Engineering is about applying those ideas to solve real-world problems. There's a great deal of overlap, as NGSS and the *Science Framework*'s authors recognized. And even though we may initially be intimidated by the idea of adding engineering into science, the truth is that Grade 3–8 teachers have successfully taught similar investigation activities for generations. Beside building structures in this chapter, and lighting bulbs in Chapter 2, if you think about it students are solving engineering-like problems in this book's activities when making clay "boats" float and even when investigating ideas about designing habitats for pillbugs (or any other living things). I didn't realize I would have so many engineering-like activities in this book when I started. Full confession, I didn't plan it that way. If you think about investigation activities you or other teachers you know have done, you may similarly discover elements of the engineering design process have been part of your professional life for years!

Additional Resources

To learn more about structures, useful websites include The Exploratorium's www.exploratorium.edu/structures/ and the straw bridges investigation activity from the Integrated Teaching and Learning Program at the University of Colorado at www.teachengineering.org/view_activity.php?url=collection/cub_/activities/cub_brid/cub_brid_lesson01_activity2.xml.

See also the following books: Zubrowski, B. (1981). Messing around with drinking straw construction: A children's museum activity book. Boston, MA: Little, Brown and Company; Zubrowski, B. (1993). Structures. White Plains, NY: Cuisenaire Company of America; Salvadori, M. (1990). The Art of Construction: Projects and Principles for Beginning Engineers & Architects. Chicago, IL: Chicago Review Press.

Chapter 9

Learning to Fish

Where do you go next?

In this chapter, you will come to see how

- open-ended investigations offer students a chance to do more of the thinking and learn more indelibly, and
- guided-inquiry is about giving your students the right amount of guidance and support they need for where they are in terms of prior knowledge and ability.

You will be able to

- compare how activities like those in this book differ from classic "cookbook" labs, and
- adapt your favorite science lessons to become more open-ended and powerful, to ensure students are really "doing science."

There's a famous Chinese proverb that says, "Give a man a fish, and you feed him for a day. Teach a man to fish, and you feed him for a lifetime." Throughout this book, I have tried to give you lots of fish—hands-on, inquiry-based activities and advice for their implementation that you can use with your students to help them better understand what science is, how science works, and how to learn, while using science's practices. But, as the book comes to a close, I recognize that only takes you so far. If you've read this far and tried some investigation activities with your students, perhaps you're ready for more. Perhaps you have other science activities that you'd like to adapt to be more like the ones in this book.

If so, then it's time for a metaphorical fishing lesson. In this chapter, I offer ideas about adapting preexisting lessons to become more open-ended. Premade lab activities are typically presented via some combination of the following:

- An *introduction*, providing background information (especially at the middle level), possibly something that's supposed to engage students and their interests, and possibly a question that's investigated in the activity
- A step-by-step *procedure*, probably numbered, telling students precisely what to do in the activity
- A premade, blank *table* (or something similar) in which students are directed to write their data; in some cases, this might include instructions for creating a graphical display of results.
- *Questions* students are expected to answer, related mostly to results they were expected to have found and conclusions they are expected to make on the basis of their data.
- Other information for the teacher, like a list of materials, suggestions for setting up the activity, answers to questions, assessments, etc.

The following activity is an example.

Pendulums

Problem: What factors or variables affect the swing of the pendulum?

Hypothesis: Write what you think will happen in Parts I, II, and III.

MATERIALS

- Pendulum bobs of different weights
- String
- Meter sticks
- Stopwatches
- Electronic balances
- Ring stands or something to hold pendulums in place

PROCEDURE

PART I

1. Determine the mass of the pendulum bob in grams. Record this value in the appropriate column of Table I.

2. Set up a 2-meter-long pendulum.

3. Center a meter stick under or next to the bob when it is at rest.

4. Displace the bob 10 cm from rest.

5. Release the bob and count the cycles made in 30 seconds. Enter your data in the first row of Table I.

6. Now displace the bob 20 cm from rest and repeat the count of cycles in 30 seconds. Enter your data in the second row of Table I.

7. Repeat for displacements of 30, 40, and 50 cms. Enter your data in the appropriate rows in Table I.

PART II

1. Displace a 20-g pendulum bob 50 cm and count the cycles for 30 seconds. Enter the bob's mass (20 g) and number of cycles in Table II.

2. Repeat the process with pendulum's whose bobs have masses of 40 g, 60 g, 80 g, and 100 g. In each trial, enter the bob's mass and number of cycles counted after 30 seconds in Table II.

PART III

1. Set up a 1.25-meter-long pendulum with a 20-g bob.

2. Displace the bob about 20 cm and count the cycles for 30 seconds. Enter your data in the first row of Table III.

3. Repeat for pendulum lengths of 1.00, 0.75, 0.50, 0.25, and 0.10 meters, entering your data in appropriate rows in Table III after each trial.

	DISPLACEMENT (CM)	MASS OF BOB (GRAMS)	LENGTH (METERS)	SWINGS (30 SECONDS)
Table I Testing for Displacement	10		2.00	
	20		2.00	
	30		2.00	
	40		2.00	
	50		2.00	
Table II Testing for Mass	50		2.00	
	50		2.00	
	50		2.00	
	50		2.00	
	50		2.00	
Table III Testing for Length	20		1.25	
	20		1.00	
	20		0.75	
	20		0.50	
	20		0.25	
	20		0.10	

Note 1: For brevity, I am leaving out the hypothetical introductory text, directions for making graphs, questions for students to answer (which hint at expected results), and teacher support information that's usually included in similar labs. Directions for Parts II and III would probably be wordier, too. I did not write this activity with the idea you would be teaching it as is!

Note 2: I also left out a diagram or drawing of an experimental setup for Part I, showing a pendulum hanging from a ring stand, with a ruler perpendicular to the pendulum string.

LEARNING SCIENCE BY DOING SCIENCE

Activity 10 might be interesting, fun, and worthwhile. So let me begin with a disclaimer: Nothing I write in the text that follows should be construed as implying there's something bad about the activity. Students can observe pendulums, follow directions, learn lab techniques, record data, learn to work with partners, and a long list of other important educational goals. But, for purposes of the goals I've been discussing throughout this book, I point out that the activity isn't real science, students are not *doing* science. When scientists are engaged in their work, they figure out the questions they are investigating, the procedures they are following to try answering their questions, what observations they need to make to create data, and what to do with that data to figure out the questions' answers. This contrasts with a "cookbook" activity, like Activity 10, where the text comes up with the questions students investigate, tells them exactly what to do to answer the questions, what to observe and how to record it, and—sometimes—even hints at what is "supposed to" happen and its meaning. In other words, students don't really have to think! They are performing demonstrations. They may be cool demonstrations, but they differ from scientific investigations.

I know what some of you are thinking now. Giving children—or even adults—materials and asking them to perform a scientific investigation is a path to chaos and failure. Open-ended inquiry-based instruction is uncommon in classrooms. Alternatives exist, however, to simply turning students loose with materials.

A STEP-BY-STEP ADAPTATION GUIDE

If you regularly engage students in hands-on activities, regardless of subject matter—if you have developed routines and classroom management procedures to succeed in busy, active classrooms—then you can take cookbook activities and *gradually* transition to more open-ended inquiry-based activities. Multiple ways exist to do this; here's one step-by-step path you can use as a starting point.

Step 1: Examine an activity, especially its introductory section, and identify the question (or questions) being answered by the procedure. Before students do the activity, introduce it to them via this question—because science is about asking and answering empirical questions, a point you can tell your students over and over throughout the year.

In Activity 10, instead of saying "today we're going to look at pendulums," for example, say something like "today we're going to find out how pendulums swing faster or slower when we change them," or "today's we're going to try to find answers to these questions," followed by writing the lab activity's question(s) on a whiteboard. Sometimes the lab's writers even include this information for you. You could even ask students to read the lab procedure before starting, and identify the question(s) it addresses, if you believe they have the skills and abilities to succeed at the task.

Parenthetically, notice how Activity 10's introduction includes a "hypothesis" asking students to write what they think will happen. As I discussed earlier, hypotheses differ from predictions, and these directions are asking students to make predictions. Personally, I suggest simply deleting the entire line. If you prefer keeping it, I suggest changing the section name to "Prediction" and encouraging students to write at least two possible outcomes for the various parts of the investigation activity, to get away from the idea science and science ability is about knowing the right answers.

Step 2: Look at the parts of the procedure where students are told what to observe and how to record their observations. Consider the idea of removing the premade chart or table for writing observations, as well as prescriptive directions telling students what, where, and how to record observations. In other words, you perform the activity *just as you would before except for omitting the table or chart.*

The end result becomes Activity 10.1.

Pendulums

Problem: What factors or variables affect the swing of the pendulum?

Materials: Pendulum bobs of different weights, string, meter sticks, stopwatches, electronic balances, ring stands, or something to hold pendulums in place

PROCEDURE

NOTE: Be sure to record your data in your notebook!

PART I How does a pendulum's displacement affect its frequency?

1. Record the mass of the pendulum bob in grams.
2. Set up a 2-meter-long pendulum
3. Center a meter stick under or next to the bob when it is at rest.
4. Displace the bob 10 cm from rest.
5. Release the bob and count the cycles made in 30 seconds.
6. Now displace the bob 20 cm from rest and repeat the count of cycles in 30 seconds.
7. Repeat for displacements of 30, 40, and 50 cms.

PART II How does a pendulum's mass affect its frequency?

1. Displace a 20-g pendulum bob 50 cm and count the cycles for 30 seconds.
2. Repeat the process with pendulum's whose bobs have masses of 40 g, 60 g, 80 g, and 100 g.

PART III How does a pendulum's length affect its frequency?

1. Set up a 1.25-meter-long pendulum with a 20-g bob.
2. Displace the bob about 20 cm and count the cycles for 30 seconds.
3. Repeat for pendulum lengths of 1.00, 0.75, 0.50, 0.25, and 0.10 meters.

You may hold a brief discussion hinting at what you want students to pay attention to, and how they might write their observations. You might remind them throughout the activity to remember to record the observations they think are important. However, refrain from being overly prescriptive; leave at least *something* about recording the data to the students' discretion. That way, when the activity is finished you can hold a productive discussion asking students to look at different ways classmates recorded their data, helping students think about the advantages of each, and having a lesson about how scientists try to display their data in ways that are clear and easy to understand.

What about students who don't record anything? Or students who record the "wrong" things? They'll probably need to repeat the activity—so choose a short activity the first time you decide to try this! After having to come back to repeat an activity, the students will hopefully remember to record data ever after.

NGSS Connection: SEP8 Obtaining, evaluating, and communicating information

What about students who don't record their data in a table like Tables I, II, and III? This presents a wonderful opportunity to discuss data collection and display, comparing the advantages and disadvantages of different ways students recorded their data. The eighth NGSS science and engineering practice is about communication. So is a discussion about ways to display data. Think of this as a language arts lesson (really). And keep in mind multiple ways exist to record or display data. The purpose of removing data tables is for students to explore and compare different ways to communicate information.

Step 3: Having taught an activity like Activity 10 without premade data tables, do it again with the next hands-on science activity you teach. We're discussing something that might be new to your students. Change takes time. You and your students can make the transition to more open-ended activities gradually and comfortably. Try something new, and then do it again and again until both you and your students feel comfortable, skilled, successful, and ready for more change.

Any student lacking prerequisite skills, attitudes, and knowledge for an activity will not learn what the teacher hopes will be learned. The student may learn nothing, learn by rote (quickly forgotten), or learn a misconception. So only take your students to a level of open-endedness you feel they are ready for.

Step 4: When your students are ready, examine the step-by-step procedure they will follow in their next hands-on science activity. See if there's one step you could tweak so students would need to figure something out on their own, something you know your students could handle. In Part I of Activity 10, for example, instead of being told (in Step 7) to displace their pendulum bobs 30, 40, and 50 centimeters, students could instead be told simply to choose three more displacements, and to repeat the procedure they've been following (recording how far they displaced their pendulums in each trial). Assuming directions related to data tables have already been removed, the only change I'm discussing here is one sentence at the beginning of Step 7; everything else about the procedure can stay the same.

Afterwards, or even during the activity, you can ask students about why they chose the displacements they did. You may, in some cases, get a window into their thinking you otherwise would not have received. Some students may choose huge displacements, and others may barely move their pendulums at all.

When class data are compared, because they'll be so varied, you'll have more to discuss with students. And students will be just a little more engaged in the activity, worrying a little less about whether they got the right answers.

Step 5: As with the change related to removing data tables, Step 4 should be repeated over and over in the next hands-on activities, with you making increasingly larger changes to the activity's procedures. Find places where you can replace a specific instruction with something slightly more general, so students will have a little discretion in figuring out what to do. Repeated enough, the day will eventually come when you look at some activity, decide your students have the requisite knowledge and skills to be successful, tell them a question to investigate, provide them with necessary materials and perhaps a brief demonstration, and leave them to figure the rest of the activity out for themselves.

If you've tried investigation activities from this book, you've already done this! For example,

- A classical version of the Milk Fireworks activity includes detailed directions telling students what to do both when initially observing a drop of detergent causing milk and food coloring to swirl, and *also* when investigating how the swirling behavior changes with cold, room temperature, and warmed milk. Instead, I advocated that most students could complete the latter activity given only the question to investigate and necessary materials.

- A cookbook version of Sinking and Floating might direct students to place objects in water in a specific order, observe whether they float, and record their observations in a provided table. I opened up that step, allowing students to follow their own curiosity and ideas a little in deciding for themselves what order to place objects in water— even though you and I are still firmly in charge of what objects are ultimately tested, by limiting materials students are provided.

- A highly directed version of Batteries and Bulbs might tell students exactly how to connect their materials to make a bulb light, or to make series and parallel circuits. My version was much more open-ended. It'll take longer for students to light bulbs this way, and they may struggle a little more. But when they succeed, they will remember what circuits are all about much better than students who weren't instructed this way!

THE GUIDED INQUIRY APPROACH

The ideas we tend to retain are those we create for ourselves. To create ideas for ourselves, we must be given the chance to do so. When you feel you and your students are ready for this kind of *guided inquiry* activity, I believe there are a few things you should consider first:

1. As their teacher, consider what you believe students need to know and be able to do in order to be successful in the modified activity. If you feel students are lacking requisite knowledge or skills, I would advocate not modifying the activity this much. The guided inquiry version of Batteries and Bulbs I discussed earlier, for example, is predicated on the belief the students will have seen or touched flashlight batteries and bulbs before the activity begins.

2. I believe you will feel most successful modifying an activity this way when the content to be learned is tangible and concrete, where students have had relevant background experiences with it. It's a point I've made throughout this book. In the open-ended Milk Fireworks activity, for example, the content to be learned is completely observable, and students would have had relevant background experiences because they already completed another version of the same activity before moving on to answering the question about milk temperature. Until you and your students start feeling comfortable with this much open-endedness, you might even restrict the activities to the end of a unit, with students extending ideas and skills you already believe they have learned.

3. Besides changing activities, it's also critical you change what you say and do while teaching the activities. Teachers' behaviors are the most important variable affecting student learning. I've tried presenting exemplars throughout this book, but two broad behavior categories probably stand out.

First, as students are working independently during activities, ask questions encouraging thinking and testing. I find it useful to keep the question stems and general questions in mind and complete the questions on the basis of students' activities. Suggestions include:

- What are you observing? (or, Tell me about what you're observing.)
- What are you thinking? (or, Tell me about what you're thinking.)
- Tell me some more about how you figured that out.
- What do you think would happen if . . . ? (or, If we were to do _____, do you think there would be more, less, or the same of _____?)
- Why do you think so?

Second, another point I've tried to make throughout the book is that simply doing hands-on science activities, even open-ended ones, does not automatically ensure kids will better understand the nature of scientific knowledge or science's practices. You, as teacher, need to make the connection explicit by showing students when they are using practices or demonstrating key ideas about what science is and how science works.

So, finally, what about a true guided inquiry version of this activity, something for students who have studied the subject, perhaps completed a similar investigation, whose teachers believe they have the requisite knowledge, skills, and experience to successfully complete it? In other words, what would a guided inquiry investigation activity of pendulum behavior, coming at the "elaboration" or "application" phase of the 5E/learning cycle be like?

Students would be given materials, perhaps a sample experimental setup of the pendulum at the front of the classroom, and the question (or directions) to investigate. Perhaps you would decide students should complete Parts I and/or II, as written, before being turned loose to complete Part III as an open-ended guided-inquiry activity.

Pendulums

Problem: What factors or variables affect the swing of the pendulum?

Materials: Pendulum bobs of different weights, string, meter sticks, stop-watches, electronic balances, ring stands or something to hold pendulums in place

PROCEDURE

NOTE: Be sure to record your data in your notebook!

PART I How does a pendulum's displacement affect its frequency?

1. Record the mass of the pendulum bob in grams.
2. Set up a 2-meter-long pendulum.
3. Center a meter stick under or next to the bob when it is at rest.
4. Displace the bob 10 cm from rest.
5. Release the bob and count the cycles made in 30 seconds.
6. Now displace the bob 20 cm from rest and repeat the count of cycles in 30 seconds.
7. Repeat for displacements of 30, 40, and 50 cms.

PART II How does a pendulum's mass affect its frequency?

Now it's your turn! Design an investigation to figure out whether a pendulum's frequency changes as the mass of the bob hanging on the end of the string increases. Use the materials provided, and don't forget to write down what you did, with enough detail that someone else could repeat your procedure, as well as the data you created!

PART III How does a pendulum's length affect its frequency?

Design an investigation to figure out whether a pendulum's frequency changes as its string gets longer. Use the materials provided, and don't forget to write down what you did, with enough detail that someone else could repeat your procedure, as well as the data you created!

Or, perhaps students would complete Part I (providing background experiences), then you would formally introduce the topic however you wished to do so, and students would then continue to Parts II and/or III. This would better approach the 5E or learning-cycle model of instruction. Part I is somewhat exploratory, formally introducing the topic is content introduction or explanation, and Parts II and III are application or expansion activities.

Either way, you might say something like, "Do you think a pendulum will swing more, less, or the same number of times in 30 seconds as its string lengthens?" Multiple responses would be solicited, always followed by "Why do you think so?" And then students would be turned loose to design investigations which they ultimately carry out. (Teachers often require students to have their procedures approved before being allowed to complete the investigations. Some teachers also require students to write about how they will record data before being allowed to begin, too.)

Walking around the room, helping students, you say things like, "tell me about what you're doing here"; "what are you thinking?"; and "what do you think will happen when you . . . ?" Investigations might differ slightly from group to group, and you could ask questions like, "How do you think [that group's] results will differ from yours?" (And "why do you think so," of course.) All sorts of discussion possibilities will be raised.

CONCLUSION

Once you get to the point where you feel comfortable teaching this way, seeing and hearing the interesting variety of things students say and do, you'll never want to go back to a classroom where everyone's doing the same thing! I appreciate the time and effort you are putting in to make this happen—and so will society, as your students move on to becoming independent, critically thinking adults. I wish you many years of interesting, happy students enjoying time spent learning about science in *your* classroom.

Appendix A

An Introduction to the Next Generation Science Standards

Science standards in the past were generally created by individual states or national organizations. If you currently teach, or were recently a K–12 student, you are probably familiar with your state's standards. Educational standards in the United States are adopted on a state-by-state basis. We have no legally binding national standards. Nevertheless, organizations have created national standards documents. Examples in science include 1996's *National Science Education Standards*, developed by the National Research Council and 1993's *Benchmarks for Science Literacy*, developed by the American Association for the Advancement of Science (AAAS).

Early in the 2010s, a consortium that included the National Research Council, AAAS, National Science Teachers Association, Achieve (a nonprofit organization involved in developing standards in other subject areas), and a consortium of about half the U.S. states developed new science standards—the *Next Generation Science Standards* (NGSS).

NGSS's supporters are interested in making common science standards in the United States, as found in many other countries. Nevertheless, each state individually adopts standards, deciding whether their science standards will be based entirely, partially, or not at all on NGSS. In my state, California, officials solicited—and received—quite a bit of public feedback before adopting a slightly customized version of NGSS as the state's science standards in 2013. You may also live in a state that has adopted NGSS as its legal standards.

NGSS differs from past science standards in a few key ways. First, NGSS addresses fewer science concepts than other standards. U.S. science standards have long been criticized for being "a mile wide and an inch deep," addressing many ideas superficially at the expense of devoting instructional time to helping students develop deeper understandings of key ideas.

The teams behind NGSS (and the National Research Council's K–12 Science Framework, the foundation document for the Standards) tried to identify science's core ideas, accenting big, explanatory ideas and ideas that might be personally or socially useful to citizens. They called these *disciplinary core ideas*. Disciplinary core ideas, or DCI's, are statements about science content that may be akin to the kinds of science standards you are accustomed to seeing. Every NGSS student performance expectation includes a disciplinary core idea.

NGSS's authors also recognized some ideas are not limited to individual science disciplines; some ideas are shared or cut across all sciences. The authors called these *crosscutting concepts*. Every NGSS student performance expectation also includes a crosscutting concept.

For purposes of this book, however, the most important difference between NGSS and past standards is an increased emphasis on the kinds of thinking constantly employed by anyone doing science, which the authors called science's practices. In addition, recognizing how often science and its use in the wider world are connected, the authors included not only science practices, but also engineering practices. Together, they called these *science and engineering practices*. Every NGSS student performance expectation includes a science and engineering practice.

Putting it together, all NGSS's performance expectations include disciplinary core ideas (DCIs), crosscutting concepts (CCCs), and science and engineering practices (SEPs). For example, one performance expectation says

Students who demonstrate understanding can:

> 5-LS2-1: Develop a model to describe the movement of matter among plants, animals, decomposers, and the environment. [Clarification Statement: Emphasis is on the idea that matter that is not food (air, water, decomposed materials in soil) is changed by plants into matter that is food. Examples of systems could include organisms, ecosystems, and the Earth.] [Assessment Boundary: Assessment does not include molecular explanations.]

Here's how to understand what it says. The content ideas within the performance expectation are about interdependent relationships within ecosystems, and how matter and energy cycle in ecosystems. The idea of a system, and describing systems in terms of their component parts, is one of NGSS's crosscutting concepts. And students being asked to develop a model to describe (and explain) what's happening in an ecosystem is one of the science and engineering practices.

I know all this because I retrieved the performance expectation from the NGSS website (www.nextgenscience.org), more specifically http://nextgenscience .org/pe/5-ls2-1-ecosystems-interactions-energy-and-dynamics. Take a look, hovering your mouse over various words in the performance expectation.

Note also how the performance expectation is labeled. It's 5-LS2-1. The "5" means it's a fifth-grade standard. Middle school performance expectations are all prefixed "MS." "LS" means it's life science, and "LS2-1" specifically refers to the *Science Framework's* LS2 core idea.

The people behind NGSS created an extensive website. The URL is www .nextgenscience.org. More information about how to read the standards is online at www.nextgenscience.org/how-to-read-the-standards. On the NGSS website, you will find useful resources about understanding the standards, their relationships to each other, how student abilities develop over time and experience, etc. The site also presents a search engine allowing you to explore the document in all sorts of ways. The National Science Teachers Association's website is also a great resource for learning more about NGSS (ngss.nsta.org).

This book, however, is not about NGSS. It's about the nature of science, NGSS's science and engineering practices, and understanding how instruction can help students understand these ideas. The eight NGSS science and engineering practices are

1. Asking Questions (for science) and Defining Problems (for engineering)
2. Developing and Using Models
3. Planning and Carrying Out Investigations
4. Analyzing and Interpreting Data
5. Using Mathematics and Computational Thinking
6. Constructing Explanations (for science) and Designing Solutions (for engineering)
7. Engaging in Argument From Evidence
8. Obtaining, Evaluating, and Communicating Information

Each NGSS performance expectation includes one of these SEPs; practices are central and vital to NGSS.

The practices themselves are discussed more fully in the NRC's *K–12 Science Framework*. As I write this, a print version of the document can be purchased, or read online free at www.nap.edu/catalog/13165/a-frame work-for-k-12-science-education-practices-crosscutting-concepts (or http:// bit.ly/292Gtx8).

Appendix B

Teacher to Teacher

Advice From Elementary and Middle School Colleagues

Throughout this book, I have discussed hands-on, inquiry-based science activities appropriate for students in Grades 3–8. Most of the activities are classics or otherwise taught often in real-life classrooms. With only minor changes, the activities work well throughout the entire third- to eighth-grade spectrum. As readers, I recognize you as skilled teachers, knowledgeable about your students, your classrooms, and the kinds of activity modifications you would need to increase the chances of student success.

Nevertheless, I also realize you might feel a little more confident with added information or guidance about teaching open-ended science activities to students in your grade levels. To help answer those questions, I went directly to the field, interviewing four of my colleagues uniquely poised to help because they regularly work with both Grade 3–5 and 6–8 teachers. This chapter summarizes what they told me.

Jill Grace is an elementary science specialist and middle school teacher, which means she's taught science at both the elementary and middle levels. She's currently mentoring other K–8 teachers learning to implement NGSS's practices as a regional director for the K–12 Alliance/WestEd. **Marissa Stillittano** and **Amy Argento** are both former teachers of the year for the Torrance Unified School District, in Torrance, California. They're currently on assignments as science resource teachers in that district. Marissa taught seventh-grade science for 10 years, and Amy taught sixth-grade science for 6 years, fifth grade for 3, and fourth grade for 1. **Susan Gomez-Zwiep** is one of my colleagues in the Science Education Department at California State University Long Beach. Susan also has extensive experience teaching both middle- and elementary-level science.

I was initially seeking information about how this book's activities differed by grade level, so I asked them questions like, "How does teaching mystery powders differ when taught to Grade 3–5 students versus 6–8 students?" All four teachers stressed similarities teaching the activities to different grades levels, however. The differences they expressed related to broader levels outside the details of individual activities.

WORKING WITH YOUNGER CHILDREN

Naturally, they notice differences between younger and older students. Differences exist, for example, in their thinking abilities. I discussed age-related cognitive differences throughout this book when writing about student expectations for applying science practices. But Jill heavily stressed the need for *both* content and behavioral expectations to be concrete, visible, and tangible with Grade 3–5 students, while she and Susan talked about Grade 6–8 students as being more varied in their thinking abilities. Older students are expected to be a little more developed in their abstract reasoning skills.

Most of the science content in this book's activities, the ideas and concepts, are pretty tangible; that's why they are appropriate for multiple grade levels. In addition, using common materials and, whenever possible, tapping into students' experiences helps make the activities less cognitively demanding as well.

Emotional differences between Grade 3–5 and 6–8 students are also readily apparent to all four teachers. Elementary students are really curious and even more enthusiastic than middle-level students. Younger children readily share their ideas, feeling less inhibited than middle school students about whether or not their ideas are "correct." This lack of inhibition fits well with the open-ended natures of this book's activities. It is great for teachers interested in understanding and responding to children's ideas, because the children share those ideas with little prompting. In fact, I think middle school teachers are sometimes jealous of the enthusiasm they see in elementary kids.

Elementary teachers know the enthusiasm, however, is accompanied by impulsiveness, short attention spans, and a great divergence of ideas being expressed. Although important to science, sometimes teachers fear this latter point, worried children will ask questions the teachers don't know how to answer. With inquiry-based instruction, however, not knowing the answer to a question often presents the chance for teacher and student to figure something out together. Questions are often investigable and a response of "I don't know. . . . Let's see if we can find out!" or "What an interesting question! How do you think we can find the answer to that?" can lead to some pretty cool explorations.

Even while elementary teachers probably spend more time redirecting students than do middle school teachers, as Susan pointed out, Marissa and

Amy repeatedly stressed how children find good, well-planned, activity-based science lessons to be extremely engaging. A question answered with "I don't know" is but a momentary distraction to a child engaged in exploring straw structures, and is certainly not a harrowing experience from the child's perspective.

Jill added a few specific suggestions of her own related to Grade 3–5 students' enthusiastic, impulsive, distractible nature when it comes to teaching science. She advises a prelaboratory lesson that's fast yet clear and simple, not burdened with lots of rules and presentations, so that those short attention spans can get going. Once instructed to connect a battery, bulb, and wire to make the bulb light, perhaps with a brief discussion about ideas students have about how to make that happen, for example, students (already trained in proper laboratory behaviors) can get right to work!

To get kids used to having materials out and available at individual work tables, without being overly distracted by the materials, she also suggested always having something out early in the school year to teach whatever lessons need to be taught about how to deal with materials, while simultaneously getting students used to having stuff out so they learn.

Teachers should similarly think through how to distribute materials to students as quickly and efficiently as possible. If all the materials a group will need are in a tub or small container, a selected student can grab the container for the groups. If watching ice melt on different materials, for example, the teacher could make up tubs with blocks of metal, plastic, a cup of ice cubes, and paper towels (for clean-up) ahead of time, call one student from each classroom table to get the group's materials, and get students working independently quickly. The "materials distributors" are preselected, chosen specifically by teacher or by some seat-related system, for example, the seat with the "yellow dot." (Although Jill was talking about Grade 3–5 students, the point applies just as strongly to 6–8 students.)

If one part of an activity is slightly more unsafe than the rest, teachers can have a station where they directly supervise students when performing the activity. In Mystery Powders, for example, an activity involving a lit tealight candle might be performed only at one station under the supervision of a teacher (or perhaps another adult volunteer in the classroom). Finally, on the other end of the attention spectrum, Jill also noted the value in *not* removing materials children are still observing or otherwise fascinated by, if at all possible.

Susan added that Grade 3–5 student expectations for communication differ from those for Grade 6–8 students. Non-written communication is more common with the younger students, like talking about results or summarizing data together in a big chart or table. Older students typically have higher expectations for recording, summarizing, and communicating their thinking via writing. Whatever grade levels you may be teaching, in an era when writing and communication skills are stressed and assessed at multiple levels, I am certain you are aware of your school or community's expectations about how your students should be communicating, so I won't expand on the point here.

DIFFERENTIATED INSTRUCTION AND THE USE OF INSTRUCTIONAL STATIONS

Elementary and middle school teachers must both work within very diverse classroom settings. Educators discuss accommodating these differences so much that in some districts differentiated instruction seems to imply not only a concept, but a particular set of teacher behaviors or pedagogical approaches. And among those approaches, the use of instructional stations seems to be one of the more common ones employed during science instruction. Marissa, Amy, and Jill all discussed it.

Amy, for example, discussed at length classroom activities with students working in stations and the activities differentiated for student ability levels via "differentiation cards." They're literal cards, perhaps even laminated ahead of time, for students approaching an activity from different levels. "Helper cards" provides hints or tips some students may want for starting the activity. "Extension 1 cards" provide an additional activity for students finishing early, and "Extension 2 cards" provide a challenging activity for those finished with the activity and its extension. The tasks are set so the majority of students will complete the Extension 1 activity.

As a listener, my first thought was the technique would require a lot of work! Amy and Marissa pointed out, though, that one does not *always* need to have three cards for every station; sometimes there might be just one extension activity, for example. They also pointed out that extensions are sometimes questions to answer—like the "exit tickets" so popular in K–12 classrooms—rather than entirely new activities. That made the concept seem more realistic to me, as did the recognition that not *every* activity must have extensions, etc. It's a suggestion for some activities, not a rule to be followed for every activity. Further, some stations may be duplicates of others. A classroom with 10 stations might only have five unique stations, with each one duplicated.

In an activity like Sinking and Floating, for example, when students are shaping a piece of clay to make it float, a helper card might encourage students to try molding clay into a bowl shape or suggest they make their clay thin when testing whether various shapes will float. An extension activity might challenge students to make a "boat" that can hold a given amount of weight, and a second extension activity might challenge students to make an object that is simply suspended in water, neither floating nor sinking, like a submerged submarine standing still in the water. Because this activity takes longer than simply placing objects in water and predicting whether or not they will float, students spend more time at the station, and it might be worth having multiple stations with clay so they don't all bunch up together.

Because stations are so widespread in elementary school science, especially when teachers have issues related to insufficient materials for all students, I asked Amy and Marissa about common fears holding teachers back from experimenting with stations. On the issue of insufficient space for stations, they told me the issue can be addressed with a little creativity. Stations can be on bookshelves, student desks (if the desks are in groups), the floor, and even outside the classroom—kids can go outside, go to the cafeteria, etc. This jibes with the way Jill treats the entire classroom as a laboratory on days when students are performing open-ended hands-on activities. She may keep students outside the classroom door, preparing them for the special circumstances of working in "the lab," like they are entering a special, privileged space (which includes new behavioral expectations).

I think some Grade 3–5 teachers may also fear all the movement in the classroom, if the teacher and students aren't used to this. "Kids will be moving around and messing around and I can't control them. There's only one of me. I can't be everywhere!" For this issue my experts recommended starting small, trying stations with a subject in which you feel comfortable. Or trying stations in science, but starting with a gallery walk, where the stations are photos students answer questions about. For example, in the activity where students examine photos of animal skulls, predicting whether the animals are carnivores or herbivores, the photos could be spread around the classroom with students given one minute to look at a photo, decide if they think it's from a carnivore or herbivore, and write what they saw leading them to their conclusions. After 1 minute, the teacher makes everyone rotate to the next station. Students who don't finish can come back later (after lunch, etc.) or even take photos down to look at later.

Jill mentioned another variation, where some fraction of the class (say one-third) are at a station with the teacher, while the rest of the students are engaged in independent seat work.

From a management perspective, everyone agreed it was important that group sizes and tasks be assigned in ways such that there were enough materials and groups were small enough that *every* student had something to do at all times. When students are engaged in tasks they feel capable of completing, and they understand what they are supposed to be doing, behavioral problems diminish. You already know that!

The part you may be less aware of comes from adding in students having some choices in what they are doing—which always happens in somewhat open-ended hands-on science activities. If the other conditions are present (clear directions, students understanding and feeling capable, sufficient materials, everyone having something to do), behavioral problems diminish even further and the classroom becomes even happier and more productive. (Or, if opening things up this way feels a little intimidating, choices can be made at the group level rather than individuals. Teams can try to reach consensus or, if necessary, make their ultimate decision the old-fashioned way—rock, paper, scissors.)

WORKING WITH MIDDLE SCHOOL CHILDREN

Turning specifically to middle school, Susan, Jill, Marissa, and Amy all described Grades 6–8 children as being more sophisticated than younger children, but also more complacent. They think a little more abstractly than younger children and communicate with more sophisticated language. They also learn from text more readily than younger children. But, by the time they reach Grades 6–8, children often have become accustomed to direct instruction. Following rules, getting "right answers," and avoiding trouble by doing what the teacher expects are high on their list of in school concerns. Middle school teachers hear questions like "How long do we have?"; "What are the rules?"; "Are we allowed to . . . ?"; "Is it OK to do. . . ?"; "Am I doing this right?" Where younger children pay attention to anything and everything, older children pay attention to each other and depend upon the teacher.

So some of the challenges to middle school teachers interested in inquiry-based instruction relate to helping students learn to do things by and for themselves, and tapping into the curiosity they still have. Marissa, Amy, and Jill each mentioned asking questions or statements as important ways to draw out students' curiosities. "What do you think would happen if . . . ?"; "How do you think we might <do> . . . ?"; "What do you think should come next?" are all examples of questions middle school-aged children can often handle, which simultaneously helps draw out their curiosity. (Meanwhile, I have stressed the value of similar questions throughout this book as starting points for helping students understand what science is and how science works. Asking, "what do you think would happen if" questions taps into curiosity, following up with a statement about how scientists make and test predictions reinforces a lesson about how science works.)

To help develop students' independence, not always relying on the teacher for confirmation or directions, Jill mentioned simply not always answering questions or problems for students—instead suggesting they figure out a solution on their own—and rewarding or recognizing the students when they have struggled, whether they succeeded or not. She also pointed out the advantages to teachers in not rewarding work simply because it's "pretty," as in a child spending hours carefully coloring a picture and then being rewarded for his or her attractive results. Some of the messy papers can get just as much credit, too.

Finally, early adolescents—especially boys becoming accustomed to their new bodies—sometimes treat materials rather harshly. Any middle school teacher or parent who has seen kids slam notebooks down understands this point. This is not always great for the materials, so Jill pointed out the need to instruct and reinforce students in how to move carefully through the laboratory and always treat materials gently.

WORKING TOGETHER

In my conversations, I was also struck by the importance everyone placed on students learning to work together productively and maturely in groups. Grade 3–5 students have issues from one student in a group taking over and being bossy, as well as the tears that can come when feelings are hurt. Grade 6–8 students have issues from off-task behavior, students fooling around, and students paying more attention to each other than instructional tasks. And students of both ages can have issues when one student "mooches" off the rest, doing little or no work, possibly diminishing an activity's value to others.

Each person also talked about the need to train students to work together, how they need instruction, practice, more practice, and reinforcement to help them develop social skills and collaboration skills to work together cooperatively and productively. Managing materials and tasks to make sure each student has something important and specific to do helps a lot (as does giving each child a different color to write with, which permits monitoring each individual's contributions). Jill discussed roles students can be assigned in groups, like having a single person responsible for getting or putting away materials, or allowing only one person in each group to ask questions of the teacher (accenting how assigning this "communicator" role can decrease the demands on teachers when lots of students are asking questions and vying for their attention). But, through it all, training and retraining are still vital. Persevering to make the skills routine pays off. The skills can be learned within lessons in any subject areas, not just science, and their values transcend school. We *all* need to know how to get along and work together for success in life as well as school. Jill put it this way:

> I do think it's worth it for teachers to hear that the struggle is worth it, especially when having kids work in teams and needing to communicate with each other. Things may not go as you planned the first couple times, kids may goof off, but given time, students will usually exceed your expectations. When this happens, the learning that comes from the collaboration is extraordinary.

CLASSROOM MANAGEMENT

Although my colleagues discussed cognitive and emotional differences between upper-elementary and middle school children, differentiating instruction, and group work, it was clear to me the key skills prerequisite to success in activity-based science related to classroom management. If you have a **good lesson,** with **clear directions** students understand and **feel capable of completing,** with **sufficient materials** and **everyone having something to do,** then you and your students are going to have a good day!

Here, however, are seven specific management suggestions my experts noted:

Use and practice using an *attention signal* when you want students to transition from working independently with materials to paying attention to the teacher. In the case of inquiry-based science this seems to often include an action where students literally take their hands off the materials (hands on the table, or in the air, or on their shoulders, etc.).

Teach students *time management*. As activities progress, warn students a few minutes before they will be moving on to something else. Project a timer for students to monitor.

Think proactively. Think through an activity, anticipating places where students might behave inappropriately and see if materials can be structured to minimize the probability of misbehavior. Similar thinking can be used for grouping students. The best way to deal with problems is to figure out how to avoid them in the first place. If you anticipate a few students would use food coloring inappropriately during the Milk Fireworks activity, structure the activity so *other* students handle the material, and it's not passed out until it's needed.

Catch them being good. Correcting misbehavior only goes so far. Recognizing expected behaviors, even calling parents to let them know, has more long-lasting effects than trying to change misbehavior.

Communicate *clear expectations*. Students can only behave properly if they know exactly what that means. Children understand science ideas concretely and tangibly—and they often understand teacher expectations the same way. Expectations should be clear, described via observables, few in number, and repeated often.

Make routines routine. Along the same lines, routines should not only be taught but used extensively, predictably, and daily (especially for absent minded middle school students). If the teacher has a special routine for transitioning from whole-group work to laboratory activities, for example, students should be taught the routine, practice it, be recognized for meeting expectations, and then the same routine should be used at the beginning of all laboratory activities.

Model new skills before students go on to practice them. Help students see and hear what they are expected to do, rather than only communicating the ideas verbally. It's all about clarity. If students working with Mystery Powders have never used eye droppers before, show them how it's done, maybe even have them practice with water before moving on to the activity itself.

Everyone I spoke to agreed transitioning to new instructional methods takes time. Sometimes it takes patience, too. I tried to show you how to transition slowly in another appendix, but I recognize open-ended, inquiry-based science to help students learn about the nature of science and science practices can be a bit daunting for a few weeks.

Once you get the hang of it, though, once you see how excited and engaged students get during the activities, once you see how much more interesting, fun, engaging, and ultimately easier—that's right, easier—it is to teach good open-ended activities than cookbook procedures, you will never want to go back again!

Enjoy the journey.

Glossary

5E model: an updated version of the learning-cycle model of instruction, adding explicit instructional phases for engaging students' attention and evaluating their learning; usually discussed in terms of its five instructional phases—Engage, Explore, Explain, Elaborate, Evaluate. See also *learning-cycle instructional model.*

Categorical variable: variables with two or more categories, and no inherent order to the categories.

Conceptual change: a model defining learning as the process of changing preconceived ideas about how the world works; usually discussed in terms of learners changing ideas, frameworks, or mental models to better align with current scientific understandings.

Continuous variable: see *numeric variable.*

Controlled variables: in an experiment, controlled variables are factors the experimenter consciously keeps the same to ensure a fair test; ideally, the independent variable is the only difference between groups being tested.

Crosscutting concepts: the overarching ideas shaping the worldview or framework NGSS's authors believe scientists use when understanding the natural world.

Deductive reasoning: the activity of using well established general premises to create more specific conclusions; often used when testing explanations by making predictions about specific situations.

Demarcation problem: the philosophical issue of distinguishing what is and is not science.

Dependent variable: in an experiment, the dependent variable is the measurement or observation being recorded as a result of changing the independent variable; it's the experiment's outcome data.

Disciplinary core ideas: the concepts or ideas NGSS's authors believe everyone should know and understand; NGSS's content core.

Discrepant event: a demonstration that produces an unexpected outcome, something differing from what students' previous experiences would lead them to believe was true.

Empirical evidence: the kind of evidence that comes from the senses—seeing, smelling, listening, etc.; often referred to as synonymous with data.

Fair test: a controlled scientific investigation; an investigation where the experimenter strives to keep all variables the same other than the one being investigated. Differences in the dependent variable can then be attributed to the independent variable.

Hypotheses: investigable scientific claims; they can be theory-like explanations or law-like generalizations.

Indirect evidence: evidence establishing a conclusion only when combined with one or more inferences; also called circumstantial evidence. All evidence other than direct eyewitness observations is considered indirect.

Independent variable: in an experiment, the independent variable is the factor the experimenter is consciously changing or testing, it's the thing he or she is trying to find out about.

Inductive reasoning: the activity of using details, observations, and other information to make or infer a generalization.

Interval data: see *numeric data.*

Learning cycle: an instructional model in which students explore ideas before being formally introduced to them, and then use their learning in new contexts afterwards; usually discussed in terms of exploration, content introduction, and application instructional phases.

Nominal variable: see *categorical variable.*

Numeric variable: variables that are number measurements.

Operational questions: questions that can be investigated and answered directly with evidence from an investigation.

Ordered variable: variables with separate categories, but an inherent order to the categories.

Ordinal variable: see *ordered variable.*

Phenomena: things in the natural world that can we can observe and wonder about.

Randomized, controlled experiment: an experimental procedure in which test subjects are randomly assigned to various treatment or control groups; random assignment minimizes preexisting differences among experimental groups.

Ratio-level variable: see *numeric variable.*

Retrospective experiment: an experimental procedure in which researchers begin with an effect and search backward in time to find potential causes, examining differences in subjects that did and did not exhibit the effect.

Science and engineering practices: the behaviors and understandings NGSS's authors believe scientists and engineers use when investigating the natural world and solving problems; essentially the cognitive processes scientists and engineers use when doing science and engineering.

Scientific law: a generalization or description of repeated observations; laws are generalizations coming from data, while theories explain laws.

Scientific theory: a broad explanation for some aspect of the natural world; strong theories are well substantiated by their abilities to explain and accurately predict a wide range of phenomena.

References

Allen, P. (1996). *Who sank the boat?* New York, NY: The Putnam & Grosset Group.

Alters, B. J. (1997). Whose nature of science? *Journal of Research in Science Teaching, 34*(1), 39–55.

American Association for the Advancement of Science. (1993). *Benchmarks for science literacy.* New York, NY: Oxford University Press.

Bergman, D. J., & Olson, J. (2011). Got inquiry? *Science and Children, 48*(7), 44–48.

Bowen, M., & Bartley, A. (2014). *The basics of data literacy: Helping your students (and you) make sense of data.* Arlington, VA: NSTA Press.

Bybee, R. W. (1997). *Achieving scientific literacy: From purposes to practices.* Portsmouth, NH: Heinemann Educational Books.

Clough, M. P. (2007). Teaching the nature of science to secondary and post-secondary students: Questions rather than tenets. *The Pantaneto Forum, 25.* Retrieved from http://www.pantaneto.co.uk/issue25/clough.htm.

Elementary Science Study. (1968). *Teacher's guide for sink and float.* Toronto, Canada: McGraw Hill.

Elementary Science Study. (1970). *Teacher's guide for structures.* Newton, MA: Elementary Science Study.

Franklin, C., Kader, G., Mewborn, D., Moreno, J., Peck, R., Perry, M., & Scheaffer, R. (2007). *Guidelines for assessment and instruction in statistics education (GAISE) report: A pre-K–12 curriculum framework.* Alexandria, VA: American Statistical Association. Retrieved from http://www.amstat.org/education/gaise/GAISEPreK-12_Full.pdf.

Gudrais, E. (2012, November/December). Soda and violence. *Harvard Magazine,* p. 11. Retrieved from http://harvardmagazine.com/2012/11/soda-and-violence.

Keeley, P. (2013, January), Formative assessment probes: Using the p-e-o technique. *Science and Children, 50*(5), 24–26.

Lee, E. J., Cite, S., & Hanuscin, D. (2014, September) Taking the "mystery" out of argumentation. *Science and Children, 52*(1), 46–52.

Loundagin, J. 1996. The Checks Lab. Retrieved from www.indiana.edu/~ensiweb/lessons/chec.lab.html.

Marek, E. A., & Cavallo, A.M.L. (1997). *The learning cycle: Elementary school and beyond.* Portsmouth, NH: Heinemann Publishing.

McDonald, J. R. (2012). Does it sink or float? *Science Activities, 49,* 77–81.

McGrayne, S. B. (1993). *Nobel Prize women in science: Their lives, struggles, and momentous discoveries*. New York, NY: Birch Lane Press.

National Research Council. (1996). *The national science education standards*. Washington, DC: National Academy Press.

National Research Council. (2012). *A framework for K–12 science education: Practices, crosscutting concepts, and core ideas*. Committee on a Conceptual Framework for New K–12 Science Education Standards. Board on Science Education, Division of Behavioral and Social Sciences and Education. Washington, DC: The National Academies Press.

NGSS Lead States. (2013a). Appendix F of *Next generation science standards: For states, by states*. Retrieved from http://www.nextgenscience.org/sites/ngss/files/Appendix%20F%20%20Science%20and%20Engineering%20Practices%20in%20the%20NGSS%20-%20FINAL%20060513.pdf.

NGSS Lead States. (2013b). Appendix H of *Next generation science standards: For states, by states*. Retrieved from http://www.nextgenscience.org/sites/ngss/files/Appendix%20H%20-%20The%20Nature%20of%20Science%20in%20the%20Next%20Generation%20Science%20Standards%204.15.13.pdf.

NGSS Lead States. (2013c). Middle school engineering design. Retrieved from http://www.nextgenscience.org/sites/ngss/files/MS%20ETS%20Storyline%20-%20DCI%20and%20Topic-6.13.13.pdf.

Osborne, R., & Freyberg, P. (1985) *Learning in science: The implications of children's science*. Portsmouth, NH: Heinemann.

Reed, R. (2016). What about pillbugs? Pacific Northwest National Laboratory. Retrieved from http://science-ed.pnnl.gov/pals/resource/cards/pillbugs.stm.

Shipstone, D. (1985). Electricity in simple circuits. In R. Driver, E. Guesne, & A. Tiberghien (Eds.), *Children's ideas in science* (pp. 291–316). Milton Keynes: Open University Press.

Smithenry, D. W., & Kim, J. (2010, October). Beyond predictions. *Science and Children, 48*(2), 48–52.

Smith, M. U., Lederman, N. G., Bell, R. L., McComas, W. F., & Clough, M. P. (1997). How great is the disagreement about the nature of science: A response to Alters. *Journal of Research in Science Teaching, 34*(10), 1101–1103.

Watson, B., & Konicek, R. (1990). Teaching for conceptual change: Confronting children's experience. *Phi Delta Kappan, 71,* 680–685.

Wolpert, L. (1992). *The Unnatural Nature of Science: Why science does not make (common) sense*. Cambridge, MA: Harvard University Press.

Yin, Y., Tomita, M. K., & Shavelson, R. J. (2008, April). Diagnosing and dealing with student misconceptions: Floating and sinking. *Science Scope, 31*(8), 34–39.

Index

interpretation of, 115–116, 128
NGSS connections and, 110
numeric data, 125, 129
patterns/correlations and, 32, 45
probabilities, hedging language and,
116, 121
science/engineering practices and, 8, 110
Seed Germination activity and, 111–112
Seed Germination/Categorical Variable
activity and, 118–119
Seed Germination/Numeric Variable
activity and, 126–127
Seed Germination/Ordered Variable
activity and, 122–123
variability in, 115–116
See also Indirect evidence; Scientific
knowledge; Seed Germination
activity; Seed Germination/
Categorical Variable activity; Seed
Germination/Numeric Variable
activity; Seed Germination/Ordered
Variable activity
Deductive reasoning, 58–59, 97
disproving premises and, 67
problem with, 67
proving true premises and, 67
See also Inductive reasoning; Mystery
Powders activity; Scientific methods
Demarcation problem, 2
Dependent variables, 41
Disciplinary core ideas (DCIs), 162
Discrepant events, 36–37, 52

Electrical Circuits activity, 19–20
batteries, addition of, 25
conceptual change model and, 21
conductors, function of, 25
currents and, 25
direct current and, 25
direct instruction and, 23, 24
elementary classroom instruction and,
24, 28, 29
empirical data, gathering/recording of,
22–25, 22–24 (figures)
empirical evidence and, 26–27
5E instructional model and, 21
hands-on/open-ended investigations and,
26–27
insulators, function of, 25
mental models and, 22, 23, 25, 26
middle school classroom instruction and,
24, 28, 29
model development and, 28–29
NGSS connections and, 20, 23, 27–28
parallel circuits and, 24, 24 (figure)

phenomena, scientific explanation of, 25
scaffolded learning and, 22
science/engineering practices and,
23, 27–29
series circuits and, 24
students' results, comparison of, 23
teaching tips for, 22–25
voltage and, 25
See also Scientific thinking
Elementary classrooms:
Carnivore/Herbivore Identification by
Skulls activity, 72–73, 76, 77
Electrical Circuits activity and, 19–20,
24, 28, 29
Investigating Pillbugs/#1 activity and,
93–94
Investigating Pillbugs/#2 activity and, 102
Melting Ice activity and, 34–35, 40
Milk Fireworks activity and, 3–4, 10, 11
Seed Germination activity and,
111–112, 117
Seed Germination/Categorical Variable
activity and, 118–119
Seed Germination/Numeric Variable
activity and, 126–127
Seed Germination/Ordered Variable
activity and, 122–123
Sink and Float/#1 activity and, 50–51,
53, 54
Sink and Float/#2 activity and, 55
Structures activity and, 134–135,
139, 141
See also Middle school classrooms;
Teaching practice guidelines
Elementary Science Study (1968), 49
Empirical evidence, 9–10, 22–23, 78
See also Data; Indirect evidence
Engineering/technology, 131–132
elementary classroom instruction and,
139, 141
life science research, engineering
principles and, 141–144
middle school classroom instruction and,
133, 141
NGSS connections and, 132–133,
142–144
real-life problems, solutions to, 132–133,
139–140, 141
science/engineering practices and,
140–141, 142–144
Structures activity, 134–135
See also Structures activity
Experimental procedures:
case control experiments and, 105
randomized experiments and, 105, 106

A SAGE Publishing Company

Helping educators make the greatest impact

CORWIN HAS ONE MISSION: to enhance education through intentional professional learning.

We build long-term relationships with our authors, educators, clients, and associations who partner with us to develop and continuously improve the best evidence-based practices that establish and support lifelong learning.

National Science Teachers Association

The National Science Teachers Association (NSTA), founded in 1944 and headquartered in Arlington, Virginia, is the largest organization in the world committed to promoting excellence and innovation in science teaching and learning for all.